North East England
Edited by Annabel Cook

First published in Great Britain in 2008 by:
Young Writers
Remus House
Coltsfoot Drive
Peterborough
PE2 9JX
Telephone: 01733 890066
Website: www.youngwriters.co.uk

All Rights Reserved

© *Copyright Contributors 2008*

SB ISBN 978-1 84431 721 9

Foreword

Young Writers' Big Green Poetry Machine is a showcase for our nation's most brilliant young poets to share their thoughts, hopes and fears for the planet they call home.

Young Writers was established in 1991 to nurture creativity in our children and young adults, to give them an interest in poetry and an outlet to express themselves. Seeing their work in print will encourage them to keep writing as they grow, and become our poets of tomorrow.

Selecting the poems has been challenging and immensely rewarding. The effort and imagination invested by these young writers makes their poems a pleasure to enjoy reading time and time again.

Contents

Annfield Plain Junior School, Stanley
Jonathan Bell (10)	1
Jack Storey (11)	1
Amber Reay (10)	2
Michaela McDonald (10)	2
Nathan John Cox (10)	3

Bothal Middle School, Ashington
Joshua Strachan (10)	3
Jill Waddle (11), Natalie Adamson & Amy Johnston (10)	4
Sarah-Louise Walden (10)	5
Samantha Brown (11)	6
Toni Pringle (11)	6
Laurie Gillespie (11)	7
Katherine Pegg (11)	7
Stephanie Williamson & Ruth Candlish (11)	8
Ellen Thompson (11)	9
Ellie Lyall (11)	10
Matthew Bolton (10)	11
Amy Thompson & Georgia Warren (11)	12
Connor Emery (10)	12
Georgia McCormack (11)	13
Leigh-Anne Williams (10)	13
Jemma McGaughey (11)	14
Rebecca Stone (11)	14
Daniel Burns (11)	15
Alix Gibson (11) & Lauren Lewicki (10)	15
Andrew Bushby & Ryan Hill (11)	16
Jake Tomlin (11)	17
Sean Charlton (10)	18
Hannah Lightley (11)	18
Faith Pritchard (11)	19
Sarah Whittle & Kate Leah Angus (11)	19
Alexandra Gibson & Elle Dunning (11)	20
Ross McGowan (11)	21
Craig Wooldridge (11)	22
Courtney Hewitson (11)	23
Lois Mordue (11) & Katy Gibson (10)	24

Stephanie Palmer & Claire Anderson (11)	24
Scott Yeowart & Nathan Bate (11)	25
Jordan Bate (11)	25
Robert Emery (10)	26
Becky Kelly & Abbie Dodds (11)	26
Robyn Dixon & Kirstin McMillan (11)	27
Alex Page & Liam Cuttler (11)	27
Shannon Elliott (11) & Chloé Cuthbertson (10)	28

Browney Primary School, Durham

Connor Edmondson (9)	28
Jordan Blackburn	29
Lucy Stidwell (9)	29
Terence Hathaway (8)	30
Jack Stidwell (9)	30
Katy Newman	30
Aaron Reid (9)	31
Sean Atkins (9)	31
Eve Ridley (8)	31
Michael Bowey (8)	32
Matthew Holden (9)	32

Bullion Lane Primary School, Chester-le-Street

Dominic Radcliffe (10)	33
Josh Davidson & Bruce Burdon (10)	33
Jasmine Lish (10)	34
Charlotte Glassey (9)	34
Abbey Tague (10)	35
Owen Pendlington (10)	35
Jordyn Dickinson (10)	36

Cockton Hill Junior School, Bishop Auckland

Ella Nicole Smith (10)	37
Matthew Sage (10)	37
Danielle Ball (10)	38
Abbey Chester (9)	38
Steven Peverley (10)	38
Charlie Douthwaite (10)	39
Bradley Wilson-Dando (10)	39
Ryan Baker (9)	39
Bradley Elgie (10)	40

Cameron Weir (10)	40
Claire-Louise Ashford (10)	41
Aimee Hillary (9)	41
Sam Stevens (10)	42
Rebecca Breden (10)	42
Aaron Swainston (10)	43
Isobel McDonagh (10)	43
Amy Dowson (9)	44
Natasha Latcham (9)	44
Jade Paterson (10)	44
Laura Eales (9)	45
Sara Winter (10)	45
Megan Kennedy (10)	45

Durham Lane Primary School, Eaglescliffe

Nathan Dale (11)	46
Zachary McAskill (11) & Ben Llewellyn (10)	46
Grace Brown (11) & Nina Marshall (10)	47
Megan Furr (11) & Emily McGuckin (10)	47
Princedeep Randhawa & Hasnain Khan (11)	48
Liam Davis (11) & Matthew Upson (10)	48
Patrick Carroll & Graham Dodds (10)	49
Bailey Peacock Farrell & Alex Close (11)	49
Antonia Phillips, Annabelle Lamond & Shauna McGahan (11)	50
Holly Chapman & Lauren Speight (11)	51

Percy Main Primary School, North Shields

Amyleigh Stewart & Robyn Watler (11)	51

Seaburn Dene Primary School, Sunderland

Thomas Hand (11)	52
Rebecca Hargate (11)	52
Dominic Shepherd (11)	53
Denys Gardner (11)	53
Daniel Atchison (11)	54
Tom Whiffen (11)	54
Lillie Keeling (10)	55
Sam Johnson (10)	55
Jack Teasdale (11)	56
Carla Topliff (11)	57

Rebecca Louise Ridley (11)	58
Jessica Green (11)	59
Haydn Evans (11)	60
James Robson (11)	60
Adam Coombs (11)	61
Mae Heskett (10)	61
Philip Jones (11)	62
Amy Lamming (11)	63
Shelley Nicholson (11)	64
David Parnaby (10)	64
Molly Mae Lloyd (11)	65

Seaton Sluice County Middle School, Whitley Bay

Lauren Brough (11)	65
Katie Pearson (10)	66
Rachel Davison (11)	66
Jessica McCafferty (11)	67
Steven Doris (11)	67
Aimee Pearson (10)	68
Ayrton Browning (11)	69
Joseph Woods (10)	69
Jasmine Common (10)	70
Amber Wakenshaw (11)	70
Lewis Devlin (10)	71
Laura Davies (9)	71
Charlotte Harris (11)	72
Sophie Brownlee (10)	72
Evan Johnson (10)	73
Liam Carroll (10)	73
Carl Howes (11)	74
Ryan Armiger (11)	74
Olivia Jarvis (10)	75
Darcey Hannah Falconer (9)	75
Lauren Devlin (11)	76
Charlie Turney (11)	76
Emma Bentley (11)	77
Lucy Thompson (11)	77
Chloe Tweedy (10)	78
Kate Foster (11)	78
Daniel McDougal (11)	79
Christina Kelly (11)	79

Name	Score
Zoe Fox (10)	80
Carl Larmouth (10)	80
David Homer (10)	81
Jenny Marshall (10)	81
Robert Lydon (10)	82
Harry Pearson (10)	82
Michael John Maley (10)	83
Callum Martin (9)	83
Dean Leon Hindmarch (9)	83
Nathan Knight (10)	84
Jennifer Taylor (9)	84
Thomas Bushell (10)	84
Luke Whatmore (9)	85
James Cleghorn (10)	85
Adam Render (10)	85
Jordan-Lee Hall (10)	86
Jamie McCafferty (10)	86
Adam Duxfield (10)	87
Rachel Swarbrick (10)	87
Melissa Smith (10)	88
Amy Bentley (10)	88
Sarah Bennett (11)	89
Rachael Burgess (9)	89
Jessica Maley (10)	90
Chloe Miller (9)	90
Tom James Ramsay (9)	91
Robyn Connelly (10)	91
Emma Doris (9)	92
Cameron Dunbar (10)	92
Emily Clark (10)	93
Steven Simpson (10)	93
Georgia Nunn (10)	94
Kayleigh Wright (10)	94
Zoe Frances Martin (10)	95
Emily Stewart (9)	95
Joseph Dungworth (11)	96
Kelly Dawn Hilton (11)	96
Leonie Tia Stuart (10)	97
Harry Green (11)	97
Blaise Charlton-Baird (10)	98
Sean Fulton (10)	98
Kyle Hall (11)	99

Jessica Govan	99
Bridie Nicole Knights (10)	100
Scott Carlisle (10)	100
Jessica Nicole Wood (10)	101
Tammi Berresford (9)	101
Jennifer Drake-Browning (11)	102
Alannah Willis Harvey (11)	102
Jane Roberts (10)	103
Shannon Little (10)	103
Chantelle Lucas (10)	104
Christopher Kennedy (11)	104
Marcus Matthewson (11)	104
Lauren Hindmarch (11)	105
Daniel James Meredith (11)	105

The Avenue Primary School, Nunthorpe

Paul O'Malley (11)	105
Grace Forster (11)	106
Matthew Wood (11)	106
William Freeman (11)	107
Laura Simpson (11)	107
Jacob Segrave (11)	108
Rebecca Palmer (10)	108
Alex Luke Morrell (10)	109
Joe Cairns (9)	109
Matthew Bennison (11)	110
Liam Reveley-Collins (9)	110
Ethan Walker (11)	111
Labib Uddin (11)	111
Rebecca Jackson (11)	112
Matthew James Bradley (10)	113
Lucy Chambers (10)	114
Katie Iley (11)	114
Joe Morley (11)	115
Luke Goddard (10)	115
Philippa Elizabeth Stone (10)	116
Molly Ryan (9)	117
Emily Heslington (10)	118
Rebecca Anne Moy (10)	118
Alexa Jayne Singleton (9)	119
Abbie May Rodgers (10)	119

Rachel Harrison (10)	120
Ryan Derek Emmerson Iley (11)	121
Shafik Rehman (11)	122
Bethany Taylor (11)	123

Trimdon Junior School, Trimdon Village
Kaitlin Behan (10)	124
Laura Robson-Cross (8)	124
Beth Donaldson & Ellie-Mae Flint (11)	125
Sophie Storey (8)	125
Laura-Beth Mitchell (10)	126
Lucy Atkinson (10)	126

Whinstone Primary School, Ingleby Barwick
Ben Pearson (10)	127
Jamie Connor (11)	127
Brett Hessing (11)	128
Callum Frost & Joe Caygill (11)	128
Charlie Scales (11)	129
Jack Bankhurst (10)	129
Olivia Rich (11)	130
James Raymond Knott (11)	130
Joseph Tomlin (11)	130
Jack Horrocks (11)	131
Abbie Manning (11)	131
Jack Christopher Thrower (11)	131
Georgia Helliwell (10)	132
Zack Thomas (11)	132
Jordan Martin (11)	133
Evie Hollis (11)	133
Sophie Patterson (11)	134
Sarah McCarthy (11)	134
Amber Khan (11)	135
Abdul Hamid Rauf (10)	135
Sonia Mansouri (11)	136
Corinne Kerr (10)	136
Daisy Hearfield (11)	137
Mathew Clasper (10)	137
Rachel Stabler (11)	138
Ben Doherty (11)	138
Luke Parkin (11)	139

Bethany Clay (11)	139
Fenella Pinkney (11)	140
Mariko Yanagisawa (11)	140
Daniel Gavaghan (11)	141
Grace Autumn Patricia Riley (11)	141
Jay Collier (10)	142
Christopher Dodds (11)	142
Logan Brennan (10)	142
Sonia Hussein (11)	143
Danny Barry (11)	143

The Poems

Being Homeless

Being homeless must be really horrible.
I can't imagine how bad it would be.
How would you feel without somewhere to sleep?
Next time you pass a homeless person by
Just take a moment to think that it could be you.

Being homeless must be really hard
I can't imagine how dirty I'd feel.
How would you feel without somewhere to wash?
Next time you pass a homeless person by
Just take a moment to think that it could be you.

Being homeless must be really harsh.
I can't imagine how hungry I'd feel.
How would you feel if you had nothing to eat?
Next time you pass a homeless person by
Just take a moment to think that it could be us.

Jonathan Bell (10)
Annfield Plain Junior School, Stanley

Litter

Pick up that litter on the road!
Get out of the littering mode.
Put those packets in the bin,
That's the big metal tin.

To be honest I'm very sad,
Dropping litter is really bad.
Please stop dropping everything,
Packets of crisps to a piece of string.

So next time you finish something,
Just think of the environment
And put it in the bin.

Jack Storey (11)
Annfield Plain Junior School, Stanley

Mum Can I?

'Mum can I have some more shoes?'
'Steve I don't know what to do,
We haven't any money.'

'Mum can I have some sweets?'
'Steve I don't know what to do,
We haven't any money.'

'Mum can we go on holiday?'
'Steve I don't know what to do,
We haven't any money.'

'Mum I haven't got the things my friends have got.'
'Steve she must feel so upset,
We haven't any money to do that.'

Amber Reay (10)
Annfield Plain Junior School, Stanley

Homeless

Being homeless - really sad.
Living on the streets - really bad.
People sleeping in rags among the rats.
My kids looking in store windows,
Saying, 'Can I have that?'
Knowing I've no money to spare.
People staring at you,
Giving you the evil eye.
Sleeping in bus stops,
Being cold and wet.
How did it happen?
What went wrong?
Will nobody see?
Will nobody help?

Michaela McDonald (10)
Annfield Plain Junior School, Stanley

Homeless

Being homeless must be hard
With no money, no one to care
Everybody turns and stares as if they do not care
Sleeping in rags they must be cold
With all the rats coming to have a nibble
Next time you pass by, think what you could do
Whether to help or just pass by
All of the homeless must just sigh
The people who pass must give the homeless the evil eye
Crying and sobbing, what a shame
Please could you help *today!*

Nathan John Cox (10)
Annfield Plain Junior School, Stanley

The Rainforests

The rainforests are dying,
Once beautiful places.
Where wildlife lived and breathed,
Untouched by Man's greed.

But now animals suffer,
And rainforests cry.
Anger in the trees,
Sadness in animals' eyes.

Man now cuts down the home
Of already endangered animals.
Torturing them continuously,
Destroying wildlife's beauty.
Why can't Man just leave them alone?
Leave them alone.

Joshua Strachan (10)
Bothal Middle School, Ashington

The Green Class

There's a boy named Michael,
He likes to recycle
Everything he can,
To help save Man,
Let's go green . . . know what I mean?

His babysitter
Never drops litter,
Let's go green . . . know what I mean?

A girl named Claire,
She air dries her hair,
To save the ozone layer,
Let's go green . . . know what I mean?

Claire has a niece,
Who wishes for peace,
Ban the bomb,
You know it's wrong,
Let's go green . . . know what I mean?

There's a boy named John,
He has a solution,
A solution to stop pollution,
Let's go green . . . know what I mean?

Call the RSPCA,
To save animals from dismay,
And to make animal abusers pay,
Let's go green . . . know what I mean?

Jill Waddle (11), Natalie Adamson & Amy Johnston (10)
Bothal Middle School, Ashington

Deadly Humans

The Earth trusted us
with all its might
but now we're a terrible sight.

The icebergs are melting,
the polar bears are dying,
people are killing them
but everyone is lying.

The past hangs in the shadows,
the world ugly and dim,
the stars are still fading,
the future looks very grim.

The world is hurting,
we are cutting down its trees,
it is bruising the environment
but no one ever sees.

How we live affects the world
and its people too,
but we aren't doing anything about it,
keeping animals in zoos.

So please help the world
to keep the human race,
so help the animals,
we have the future to face.

Sarah-Louise Walden (10)
Bothal Middle School, Ashington

My Once Beautiful Earth

My once colourful world has been smothered in fuels.
My once blue oceans have become black with oil.
My once green grass has become yellow with heat.
My once solid ice caps have become liquid with global warming.
My once happy children have become hungered with poverty.
My once tropical fish are dying out because of fishermen.
My once sensible humans: where have you been?

Samantha Brown (11)
Bothal Middle School, Ashington

Dear Humans

Dear humans,
I am a shark,
Determined to live,
But as time goes on we give and give.
Before you came,
We lived in fame,
But now we face extinction.

You think we are so nasty,
We don't want half of your cheese pasty,
You take our oil,
Is that really loyal?
But now we face extinction.

Waste, food and much, much more,
In our lives that's against the law.
Pollution, pollution everywhere,
Why can't we all just share?
That way we will all live happily.

Toni Pringle (11)
Bothal Middle School, Ashington

We Humans

Animals flee their homes as they are destroyed
People destroy them
We destroy them.

There was no fear until people stole and killed
People stole and killed
We stole and killed.

Therefore we can help them rebuild their lives
People rebuild their lives
We can rebuild lives.

Laurie Gillespie (11)
Bothal Middle School, Ashington

If Everyone Cared

God looks down
With a frown.

He says, 'Oh this will never do.'
He is so disappointed with you.

'Look at my sea
Turning black from your oil.

Look at my animals
Fleeing from their homes.

And where are my trees?
They seem to be gone.

Leave my seas
Leave my animals
Leave my trees
Leave my Earth
You've destroyed enough!'

Katherine Pegg (11)
Bothal Middle School, Ashington

I've Got A Cold

I've got a cold,
It's all because of you,
Because of the everyday activities,
That you do.

I've reached a certain point,
Where I can't take it anymore,
If you don't do something now,
I will be no more.

You may be sitting reading this poem,
Thinking, *I'm just a child, what can I do?*
Surely I can't be the cause of this awful illness
That is infecting you?

For this type of illness,
There is only one cure,
To stop global warming,
For that I am sure.

Stop dropping rubbish
And dumping oil in our seas,
Because every piece of litter that you drop
Is infecting me.

All I ask is to live peacefully,
In a land of glorious green hills
And clear tranquil seas,
So be appreciative and mend your ways
And show some respect for me!

Stephanie Williamson & Ruth Candlish (11)
Bothal Middle School, Ashington

World Destruction

Animals are dying
Fear-stricken in their eyes
Fleeing from the hunter
Who comes with other guys

The marine world is filled with colour
But soon will only be blue
As the fish are dying out
What are we to do?

Rainforests are filled with anger
With sadness and despair
The animals once trusted us
But now we threaten their lair

We're cutting down the trees
Polluting all the oceans
Destroying the ozone layer
Think of the world's emotions

We have the power to stop
But just don't realise it yet
Stop using real animal skin
Stop using large fishermen's net

So stop destroying the world
And make it a better place
There's no turning back now
So let's just close the case.

Ellen Thompson (11)
Bothal Middle School, Ashington

Poison

Poison, poison in the air
Killing land and sea
Poison, poison, no one cares
Can't anyone see?

Hunting, hunting just for sport
Wiping out species carelessly
Hunting, hunting at the port
Could be fishing illegally.

Factories, factories doubling sadly
I wish wildlife was
Factories, factories, pollution spreading badly
People say, 'It's just cos . . .'

Nature, nature slowly dying
Well, it seems to be dying fast
Nature, nature loudly crying
The amount of nature dying is vast.

Extinction, extinction, tragic but true
Cruelly killing species before they're discovered
Extinction, extinction, it could happen to you
Destroying secrets before uncovered.

Murderer! Murderer! We're all pointing at you
It's all your fault, it's what you've done
Murderer! Murderer! Extinction is no myth, it's true
It's all your fault, what have you become?

Poison, poison in the air
Killing land and sea
Poison, poison, no one cares
Can't anyone see?

Can you?

Ellie Lyall (11)
Bothal Middle School, Ashington

What's Wrong With Us?

What's wrong with us,
We've lost Earth's trust.
He's getting angry,
Warmer and warmer.

Volcanoes erupt,
The temperature's upped.
So get out of your car
And go for a walk.

Crops can't survive heat,
Neither can grown wheat.
If nothing happens now,
Earth dies unhappily.

Lava that can kill us,
Lies in Earth's strong crust.
When he explodes in anger
He will take us with him.

Scientists do think,
That Earth's on his brink.
Coming to the end,
Of a once great friendship.

Battling through is Sun,
Making animals run.
Looking for some shade,
What we do is bathe.

If you own an SUV,
Go and buy yourself a Mini.
It makes Earth happier,
So do him a favour.

Matthew Bolton (10)
Bothal Middle School, Ashington

Global Warming

Global warming will affect the world in many ways
It will kill all the plants and leave forests empty
No animals left
So nature no more
Not an animal or berry will be seen at all.

The weather so hot
Nobody can bear it
The sun so bright
Children don't care for it
Suntan cream is a must
As you could burn
The sky so blue
All you can see is an orange ball burn
That lets light shine down on the world.

It is so hot you feel tired
Our resources running low
As the temperature rises
The more you want it to go.

So help to save our world and make it great
As in the end it is your place to live.

Amy Thompson & Georgia Warren (11)
Bothal Middle School, Ashington

Out On The Street

Out on the street,
Nowhere to go.
Cold through to the bone,
No blankets to keep warm.
No families to support you,
No home to be like a family.

Connor Emery (10)
Bothal Middle School, Ashington

Wasting The Only World

Paper for doodling, paper for notes,
Paper for poems that are written by poets,
Paper is from trees that were carelessly cut,
For you to use, please look, please look.

Rubbish is dumped, rubbish like old shoes,
Rubbish which was once actually used,
Rubbish from us that was dumped in the ground,
The rubbish from you, look at those mounds.

Ice is melting very fast,
Ice which unfortunately will not last,
Ice that's now melted to freezing water,
From you driving your car, I saw ya, I saw ya.

So look after this world,
We won't get another,
Treat it with love and respect,
Tell this to your sisters and brothers.

Everyone can help,
Everyone.

Georgia McCormack (11)
Bothal Middle School, Ashington

Please Stop It

There are no butterflies in the sky,
Please stop pollution
Because everyone's sad
With their mum and dad.
Please don't litter,
That makes you bitter.
If you find litter on the ground
Put it in the bin
Near where you found.

Leigh-Anne Williams (10)
Bothal Middle School, Ashington

The Once-Loved Earth

Once the Earth was beautiful and calm,
Now it's covered with danger and harm.

The jewelled grass comforted my feet,
The peaceful daisies waved to greet.
The trees were fantastic; broad and light,
It was amazing to tiptoe through the sunlight.

Now the world is polluted and sad.
Unhappy, I am no longer glad,
That I live on this Earth.

I don't walk on the grass (it's dull and weak!)
I don't walk in the sunlight (it's hard to seek!)

You really have to help the Earth,
The consequences, you know what they're worth.

Jemma McGaughey (11)
Bothal Middle School, Ashington

Big Green Death

Big green death, smoking up the land,
Stop the factories, smoke should be banned.

Big green death, spreading over the sea,
God please help us, please help me.

Big green death, killing the trees,
Open a door to freshness, with environmental keys.

Big green death, has to stop,
Do we need an enviro cop?

Big green death, destroying their homes,
Poor little creatures, listen to their moans.

Big green death, is killing our world,
Help the environment, reduce, reuse, recycle.

Rebecca Stone (11)
Bothal Middle School, Ashington

Dumping's Happening Everywhere

Dumping here
Dumping there
Dumping's happening everywhere!

In the streets
In the sea
Can't anyone see?

Rivers dingy
Seas black
I really wish I could turn time back.

Dumping here
Dumping there
Dumping's happening everywhere!

People don't know what they're doing
People do it without a care
Now some animals are becoming rare!

Dumping is happening *everywhere!*

Daniel Burns (11)
Bothal Middle School, Ashington

Litter

L ittering is bad,
I t can make people sad,
T he people can stop littering,
T hen the world will start glittering,
E veryone will be glad,
R ejoicing and not mad.

Alix Gibson (11) & Lauren Lewicki (10)
Bothal Middle School, Ashington

Life On Earth

The Earth is increasing in heat
So come on, get off your feet.
Please don't use the car
Because you can walk very far.

Try to stop the litter
And try to be fitter.
There are lots of animals dying,
There is not a lot in the air that is flying.

There are rainforests being cut down
So come on, don't just frown.
Shut all the doors
On these *wars!*

The Earth is increasing in heat
So come on, get off your feet.
Please don't use the car
Because you can walk very far.

People are getting disease
They are in need.
Please will you recycle
And carry on the Earth's healthy cycle.

Climate change is happening
And it does not look promising.
Everybody stop pollution
So we can carry on evolution.

Andrew Bushby & Ryan Hill (11)
Bothal Middle School, Ashington

So What Should We Do?

A cow creates CO_2
It comes from 4x4s too,
So what should we do?

Mares are flying
The Earth is dying
So what should we do?

Toxic waste is coming hard
From Edinburgh to Scotland Yard
So what should we do?

Stop the Iraq war
We're sending troops more and more
So what should we do?

Don't eat from a frying pan
Earth's not happy, it needs a plan
So what should we do?

As they cut down the trees
We play on Wiis and PS3s
We are using electricity
So what should we do?

People are dying in Iran
In Iraq and Pakistan
So we all need to stop this!

Jake Tomlin (11)
Bothal Middle School, Ashington

Why Should I Care?

Why should I care?
Japan's doing the damage not us!
Or are they?

Why should I sit in the dark?
China's a bigger country than us and they don't.
Should we?

Why shouldn't I waste paper?
All that talk of us wasting, it is rubbish.
We've got plenty of trees.
Haven't we?

Why should I care?
Global warming will mean hotter summers
And who cares about the polar ice caps - they're too cold.
Or are they?

Sean Charlton (10)
Bothal Middle School, Ashington

Crying

I'm crying because . . .
oil ships are leaking into my body.
I am the sea.

I'm crying because . . .
cars are breathing poisonous fumes into my body.
I am the ozone layer.

I'm crying because . . .
rubbish is in my body which could be recycled.
I am the rubbish bin.

I am the Earth
I'm crying out loud: Heed my signs
We are going down!

Hannah Lightley (11)
Bothal Middle School, Ashington

Global Warming (Why?)

Global warming (why?)
Help our forests to survive.
Factories puff out smoke -
That makes us choke!

Buy some scissors today
And cut back pollution the best way!
Endangered animals suffer every day
So please treat their habitat in a kind way.

Cutting down our trees, we've seen it all
Forests and oxygen will be no more.

Bin it or recycle it but think, do we need it?
Waste has deadly consequences;
Our resources are running low!

Faith Pritchard (11)
Bothal Middle School, Ashington

Animals In Danger

Orang-utans swing from tree to tree
Then all of a sudden, what can I see?
It's all our fault what we can see,
Orang-utans are dying, what could this be?
It's called extinction, everybody knows,
The animals are suffering these highs and lows.
Whales are suffering and rhinos too,
Please just tell me what to do!
Don't pollute the air as much,
Because animals will die,
Many birds as such.
Habitats are being destroyed too,
We all know it's because of you!
Animals are dying out really fast,
Let's try to make all species last!

Sarah Whittle & Kate Leah Angus (11)
Bothal Middle School, Ashington

What's Happening To Our World?

We are destroying our world
with dumping waste in the lake,
pollution and litter
sooner or later, disasters we'll make!

Ice caps are melting
animals are dying,
penguins, polar bears and porpoises,
no longer in the sky will the puffins be flying.

Whales are affected too
as they live their life in the sea,
they are killed by ships and pollution,
also fishing nets, so let them free!

Recycling is simple,
it turns old things into new,
it makes a huge difference,
all of it, you can do!

We are wasting paper
and chopping down trees,
everyone boiling with ungratefulness,
from their head to their knees.

Our Earth is crying
trying to get a message to you,
'Please, treat me with respect,
stop destroying me too!'

Alexandra Gibson & Elle Dunning (11)
Bothal Middle School, Ashington

The Park Owner's Letter

Dear Council,

My park is getting out of control
Oh what shall I do?
I try to tell them kids to stop
But it just won't do.

My pond was full of fish and frogs
But now there is no more
Pollution came to say hello
Then took the fish and frogs away.

There's a boy called Michael
Who loves to recycle
He tries to tell the kids to do it too
The kids just laugh to see the chap
Oh what shall I do?

That wife of mine tells me to rest
But how can I when my park is under attack?
Please help. Oh what shall I do?
Maybe I could go help my park
From that dreadful killing shark.

Yours faithfully
Park Owner.

Ross McGowan (11)
Bothal Middle School, Ashington

Saving The Planet!

We are destroying the planet,
Now is the time to stop
Because the other countries are saving the planet
And we are not.
Everyone save the planet!

If we turn off the lights,
We could save a mile.
Go and turn off the lights,
It's well worthwhile.
Everyone save the planet!

If we turn off the taps
We could save a lake.
Save the world's waters
And pay back what we take.
Everyone save the planet!

Everyone start recycling,
Make rubbish into something new.
Just remember recycle,
It's something everyone can do.
Everyone save the planet!

Stop polluting the oceans,
The fish are dying out.
We are becoming monsters
And there is no doubt . . .
So everyone save the planet!

Craig Wooldridge (11)
Bothal Middle School, Ashington

Destroyed World

There's hardly any butterflies,
And flowers on the ground.
And with them nearly gone
There's less smiles around.
And why is this magnificent world
So sad and blue?
Well I've got a story to share with you.

There once was a beautiful world
Which had no troubles at all.
And everyone was happy,
Children sang, danced
And played with their balls.

But us disgraceful people,
Who have no respect at all
Are destroying our world, by litter,
Our seas, which means by global warming
And all the other things,
Means that less and less
Of the birds will sing.

But it's not too late to make a change
And if we act now
We might just turn our world back around
And now I've tried to tell you
With this poem that rhymes
What exactly, could happen in time.
And now I've tried to explain
What to do so the future of the world
Could be down to you.

Courtney Hewitson (11)
Bothal Middle School, Ashington

Wasted World

People are getting angry
About the damage we have done,
It's not so bad now but
It will be for your daughter or son!

Littering is the first thing
That causes the pollution,
That is so terrible
The birds will no longer sing.

Extinction is next
The birds stop to rest,
No longer will live
The creatures are perplexed!

It's recycling that turns old to new
From tins to hats and bottles to caps,
It's amazing how it works
And now it's your turn to listen and to learn.

Lois Mordue (11) & Katy Gibson (10)
Bothal Middle School, Ashington

For Let

You're throwing litter
Now the birds can't flitter
The world is foul
Now the hounds can't howl
The planet has no fate
The animals are at hate
The dinosaurs are gone
The pandas aren't - but it won't be long
The timer is set
The world is up for let
The animals are fun
But they won't be because of the sun
Apples are green, the grass is green
But, but, but the world is mean.

Stephanie Palmer & Claire Anderson (11)
Bothal Middle School, Ashington

Farewell Earth

Don't dump garbage waste
The only thing that goes in the sea is your toilet waste.

Oh no, the Earth will not last
Hurry up, go to Mars fast.

Oh God, the penguins have died
You'd said you'd help but you lied.

On the beach the seagulls are flying
Oh my god, the sea is dying.

The Earth shakes more and more
Look what you've done, I told you before.

We're on Mars now
The view on Mars is wow.

Now it's goodbye to me
I'm seeing the remainder of the Earth's sea.

Scott Yeowart & Nathan Bate (11)
Bothal Middle School, Ashington

Homeless Ain't Bad

Being homeless is not that bad
Sure you would have to wear rags
You can move home
You can even live under a garden gnome
You can fish for food
But don't be rude
But don't be sad
Even though being homeless can be a drag
Apply for a job
So you don't start a mob
Because soon you will be living the life
And there won't be another fright.

Jordan Bate (11)
Bothal Middle School, Ashington

World Elimination

The Earth is round,
The exercise is sound.
So get off your feet
And send your fleet.
So a big message says *'stop using your car*
Because you can walk very far'.

People are destroying the world.
People are destroying animals' homes.
That's why we need to let animals roam.
Trees are getting burnt, animals lose their habitat.
It's all happening here in our world.

Robert Emery (10)
Bothal Middle School, Ashington

Litter

Litter is a disgrace
It is destroying our place,
Litter is getting worse
It's like our curse.

Bottles, boxes and cans
You should pick it up with your hands,
You see it on the telly,
You see it on the ground.

People are dull
Because the bins are full,
Put it in the bin
And we will win.

We need the Earth
Please help.
Thank you!

Becky Kelly & Abbie Dodds (11)
Bothal Middle School, Ashington

Have A Heart

Children lying in the street,
No one comforts them to get to sleep,
No bedtime stories to read at night,
No good family to share their life.

Clean water, do they have?
Nice food to eat, no they don't.
Warm places to sleep, they should have.
Nobody bothers, nobody sees,
Nobody has a heart.
We can help them, those homeless children,
We'll find a way.

Some mouldy food, a tacky blanket,
Are they dreaming or is this a con?
Make them happy, have a heart,
Put a smile on their face,
Help them go back to their normal place!

Robyn Dixon & Kirstin McMillan (11)
Bothal Middle School, Ashington

Don't Leave Me Alone

The street is my home
And I live wherever I roam,
Don't leave me alone
In this dark hole,
It is so cold,
So don't leave me alone.
All I have is my pride
But it is so cold outside,
Don't leave me alone.

Alex Page & Liam Cuttler (11)
Bothal Middle School, Ashington

A Dangerous Mix-Up

Earth is crying, animals dying
Hearts are broken, no words are spoken.

I hate stepping on the ground, carbon footprints all around
Polar bears dying in the Arctic sea, why can't they live like me?

Trees are being cut down, all animals give a huge frown
And we know the prediction, they face major extinction.

Please stop pollution, we don't want a commotion
All we want is a smile, not extinction and litter every mile.

Children are crying, animals are dying
Hearts are being broken, our words have been spoken.

Shannon Elliott (11) & Chloé Cuthbertson (10)
Bothal Middle School, Ashington

Save The Planet

S ave and help this planet
A lways do your best
V olunteer your services
E veryone can help.

T he council help us recycle
H elp them sort your rubbish
E veryone can play a part.

P lease help us join our war
L itter will not win the battle
A nd to put pollution to a stop
N ever
E nding to the
T riumph against litter and more.

Connor Edmondson (9)
Browney Primary School, Durham

Walk To School

W alk to school, it is fun
A cross the path, kick the stones
L ook out for the cars on the road
K ick the stones on the path

T ouching the rusty fence, it makes me shiver
O n the path there is loads of tarmac

S uper cars going fast
C ars going past, they go very fast
H ealthy tomatoes being planted
O n the grass it is smooth
O n the way, I am nearly there
L ooking at the birds tweeting.

Jordan Blackburn
Browney Primary School, Durham

Recycling

Recycling, use the bins.
The green box is for tins.
The black one is for litter
And the green bag's for paper and card.
Use your bins, it's not very hard.
The purple van comes for the green
Which is quite mean.
Sometimes they don't collect it
That gets on my mam's nerves!
The green machine comes for the black.
Mam went mad, they nearly ran over the cat.

Lucy Stidwell (9)
Browney Primary School, Durham

Recycle

R ecycling is good for the environment and good for you.
E nvironmentally friendly our world is not!
C olourful our world is not!
Y our planet is in your hands.
C rossed over our world is.
L ovely but dull.
E nvironment, no!

Terence Hathaway (8)
Browney Primary School, Durham

Walking

W e should walk to school
A re you ready to walk everywhere? Yeah!
L earn to walk instead of cars.
K ill cars, don't waste oil, petrol and diesel.
I cebergs melting, polar bears dying because of cars!
N o to cars, no to petrol, oil and diesel.
G round rolling because of recycling.

Jack Stidwell (9)
Browney Primary School, Durham

Bins

B ins are cool because you can put rubbish in them.
I n bins you can put different things.
N ight-time people go around dumping rubbish.
S top and think before you dump.

Katy Newman
Browney Primary School, Durham

Bins

B ins help people to store rubbish.
I can save the world by recycling.
N asty people just throw rubbish on the floor.
S o let's work together to save our planet.

Aaron Reid (9)
Browney Primary School, Durham

Environment

E veryone, walk to school.
N ever be a litterbug.
V ery rarely get into a car.
I nternational recycling.
R ecycle glass, paper and card.
O riginal climate change.
N atural environment for kids.
M eaning of recycling for kids.
E nvironment take notice.
N ever let it down.
T ry to recycle.

Sean Atkins (9)
Browney Primary School, Durham

Bins

B ins are a great way to recycle.
I t is important to use a bin.
N ever throw rubbish on the floor.
S tart caring for our planet.

Eve Ridley (8)
Browney Primary School, Durham

Save Trees And Forests

S ave the environment
A nd animals
V icious people are destroying trees
E verywhere in the world.

T oday it's time for action
R ight from United Kingdom
E verywhere people are dying
E verywhere animals are dying
S ave trees today.

A dvise people to save the world
N umerous animals are endangered
D aggers are being used.

F ading away trees are soon gone
O r you can do something to help
R uining the world
E verywhere is nearly gone
S o help us today please
T oday it's time for action again
S ave forests today!

Michael Bowey (8)
Browney Primary School, Durham

Recycling

R ubbish is bad.
E lectric is good.
C ycling to school is good.
Y ou are bad if you don't recycle.
C ycle to school.
L anterns are sometimes good.
I encourage recycling.
N o rubbish.
G o recycling!

Matthew Holden (9)
Browney Primary School, Durham

Our Environment

On our planet is rock and soil,
But day by day this we spoil.

With litter and rubbish we disregard,
Living beings are finding it hard.

By killing the air that we all need,
This poem is for all that we succeed.

In making our environment a place of grace,
We must take care of our planet and space.

Dominic Radcliffe (10)
Bullion Lane Primary School, Chester-le-Street

Exhaust Fumes

Exhaust fumes are deadly,
Exhaust fumes aren't friendly,
And for what it's worth,
It's killing our Mother Earth.

We've got to try and find
A cleaner way to drive,
Or it will be too late,
There will be no one left alive.

Exhaust fumes are bad,
Don't make it more mad,
Everybody, please,
Make exhaust fumes ease.

Josh Davidson & Bruce Burdon (10)
Bullion Lane Primary School, Chester-le-Street

Crazy World

Pollution is no good . . .
Deserts where the forests stood,
Bees don't buzz, birds don't sing,
Apes and monkeys no longer swing,
No horses running in the grass,
A poisoned sea that looks like glass,
Where leaping dolphins no longer play
And giant whales stay away,
No rabbits, foxes, stoats or weasels,
A blotchy sky that looks like measles,
Dirty water that looks like blood,
That's why pollution is no good!

Jasmine Lish (10)
Bullion Lane Primary School, Chester-le-Street

Help The World

Plant a seed and watch it grow to make a happier place,
Better for me and better for you
(Stop the litter, stop the bags of rubbish)
It's more than waste, it's poison to animals,
In water and on land we must care for them all.
Think of me and think of you
We like the morning birds' song
And the owls that hoot in the dark night.
Save them while we can.

Charlotte Glassey (9)
Bullion Lane Primary School, Chester-le-Street

Environment

It's our fault water levels are rising,
We increase the temperature so the ice is dying.
When we cut the trees down it affects our population,
Not just one person, it's a whole nation.
Car fumes are in the air here, there and everywhere,
Stop the litter, stop our mistakes,
Because we are rising our rivers and lakes.

Abbey Tague (10)
Bullion Lane Primary School, Chester-le-Street

Cars

Don't use cars
Cars are bad
They do us favours
Good and sad
The saddest favour they can do
Is start polluting just like you
Pollution is bad
Pollution kills
It doesn't kill you
It kills the Earth
Pretty soon the Earth will die
So will you and so will I
So tell your parents, don't pollute
Give it the boot!

Owen Pendlington (10)
Bullion Lane Primary School, Chester-le-Street

Our World

Leaves of green,
Against a pale blue sky,
Fish that swim
And birds that fly.

Pretty little flowers,
Of yellow and pink,
How are they so beautiful?
What do you think?

Animals small
And animals big,
Some that burrow
And some that dig.

But the people that live here,
Don't seem to understand,
That everyone must
Lend a helping hand.

For very soon
You must see,
The world won't seem
Like it used to be.

The birds will be gone,
All the flowers dead,
A fire-filled sky
And faces full of dread.

No water to drink,
Or food to eat,
Hearts full of sorrow
And looks of defeat.

But we can stop it,
So lend a hand today,
And stop our lovely world,
From all turning grey.

Jordyn Dickinson (10)
Bullion Lane Primary School, Chester-le-Street

Hiding From War

So she still lies there
Poor little orphan girl,
Nobody there, nobody to care,
Shouting and screaming outside the door
Maybe she still lies there crying.
Everybody stop!
Everything destroyed,
People dying,
In a painting you don't need words to describe it.
Faces of fear, everywhere you go
We won't have it,
Everybody stop, you know it's bad, stop!
Everybody please try it
Then we won't have things destroyed,
Bombs dropped, pollution
And little children like the orphan girl,
Crying in a shelter alone with everywhere destroyed.

Ella Nicole Smith (10)
Cockton Hill Junior School, Bishop Auckland

Don't Chop And The Trees Won't Drop

Don't chop down rainforests
They look after you,
If you do you'll regret it
So don't chop down these wonderful trees,
They belong to an animal.
Would you like it if something crashed into your house?
So who's with me?
Recycle your paper and save the trees
They look after you,
So come on, we can do it.

Matthew Sage (10)
Cockton Hill Junior School, Bishop Auckland

Litter Disease!

*Reduce, reuse, recycle,
You know you want too!*

You need to know that not recycling
Is making our community a bad place to be
But you can help by recycling paper, plastic, glass,
Cans, cardboard, books and even our clothes or shoes,
Give them to a friend or a charity.
The world needs help, it is dying of illness.

Litter disease!

Danielle Ball (10)
Cockton Hill Junior School, Bishop Auckland

Useful Trees

Trees are big.
Trees are little.
Trees are very important.
Take care of trees.
Take care of trees.

They provide something very important.
They have homes for animals.
Paper for us.
So we have to take care of trees.
Take care of trees.

Abbey Chester (9)
Cockton Hill Junior School, Bishop Auckland

Trees

Don't hurt trees, they're our friends
Don't try to cut them or even make them bend
They produce oxygen that keeps us alive
Don't use too much paper or it will make them die, die, die
Don't kill trees!

Steven Peverley (10)
Cockton Hill Junior School, Bishop Auckland

Animals

We need to stop killing animals
Some animals are very rare
Stop killing whales, lions and elephants
Some animals die every day
Shot or caught in a trap.

Charlie Douthwaite (10)
Cockton Hill Junior School, Bishop Auckland

Help Trees

Trees live,
Trees die,
Trees help us survive.

Trees give us paper,
They help us to make fire,
They give us oxygen.
Don't waste paper all the time
Use paper and recycle it for another day.

Bradley Wilson-Dando (10)
Cockton Hill Junior School, Bishop Auckland

Graffiti

Graffiti is bad
It makes you feel very sad
You see it on walls
You always need to call
If you see lots of graffiti
It makes places look rough
You must act now and be real tough
Don't do it anymore
We will beat this graffiti war.

Ryan Baker (9)
Cockton Hill Junior School, Bishop Auckland

R-Reduce, R-Reuse- R-Recycle

If you don't recycle
Our planet will become a wasteland
A dump.
It will help make our world a nicer place if you can . . .
Reduce the amount of stuff you throw away.
Reuse even more stuff than you do now.
Recycle everything that you possibly can and maybe more.
You will be an RRR champion
Just like me.
And our world will be
Brilliant and beautiful.

Bradley Elgie (10)
Cockton Hill Junior School, Bishop Auckland

Trees

We can make a difference today and tomorrow,
Show you care for trees, they're helpful in every way,
If you pretend to like trees they will know what you are going to say,
If you chop them down they will fall to the ground,
So don't kill trees, they are environmentally friendly,
Be kind to trees, they are a brilliant feature of the world,
So be nice, be nice, please be very nice to trees,
They've done no harm, they help us in many ways,
They produce oxygen that keeps us running,
So please be cunning, they could make our life live longer.

Cameron Weir (10)
Cockton Hill Junior School, Bishop Auckland

Recycling

Everyone should recycle tin cans, jam jars and newspapers too.
So don't be a zero, be a hero.
Everyone should have a recycling box.
Our environment will become as clean as a whistle
So please tidy up.

Everyone should recycle.
Get your gloves on and help the planet.
Have fun and enjoy cleaning up our planet.

Claire-Louise Ashford (10)
Cockton Hill Junior School, Bishop Auckland

Tree Poem

Trees,
Help trees, they are history.
They're alive, give a tree a hug.
They are homes for animals,
We need our trees in our environment.
They help us breathe because we need oxygen
And they produce it.

So go green, grow a tree,
It will make you happy, honestly.
So make a change quickly, the trees are going,
No need to be choosy and picky with a tree,
Just go to the shop and buy any type, it really doesn't matter.
Think now, don't be greedy and cut down a rainforest,
Animals will die, be quick and save a life!

Aimee Hillary (9)
Cockton Hill Junior School, Bishop Auckland

Don't Throw Litter

Don't throw litter
You know you can do better.
Litter is a horrible thing
So put it in the bin,
Or better still, recycle it.
Don't throw rubbish,
You'll ruin the environment.
The bin is for litter.
If you do it your environment will be better.
So do your thing and put it in the bin.
You know what I mean
And we'll keep everything clean.
Don't sit there,
Just get up and clean up.

Sam Stevens (10)
Cockton Hill Junior School, Bishop Auckland

Recycling

Recycle, reduce, reuse
Paper, jars, books.
Recycle, reduce, reuse
Do it for your sake please.
Recycle, reduce, reuse
Animals need you,
They get stuck in plastic bags, cans and tins.
You can make a difference!

Rebecca Breden (10)
Cockton Hill Junior School, Bishop Auckland

Pollution

We can keep the environment a better place if . . .
We walk to school and walk more places,
We will save more plants and trees,
More animals will survive,
So when you wake up
There will be tweeting birds
Barking dogs
And when you go to the zoo
There'll be growling tigers.

Aaron Swainston (10)
Cockton Hill Junior School, Bishop Auckland

Electricity

You don't realise
but *our world* is burning out,
so when you go out
don't leave the bathroom light
dangling and wasting electricity.
From just one pull
our world can be saved!
So please all pitch in
and do your bit.
You'll make
a big difference.

Isobel McDonagh (10)
Cockton Hill Junior School, Bishop Auckland

Poor People's Poem

Poor, poor people with no homes
Children with no shoes or nice clothes
Parents beg for food and drink
So think, think, think.

Children go to no schools
They end up looking like dumb fools
Parents walk miles just for drink
So think, think, think.

Amy Dowson (9)
Cockton Hill Junior School, Bishop Auckland

Trees

Trees are precious
Trees are lovely
Trees are gorgeous
Hug trees
Don't waste paper
Just use the back
Now the trees are
Getting chopped down.

Natasha Latcham (9)
Cockton Hill Junior School, Bishop Auckland

Recycle Everyone

Go to the bin
And put your rubbish in.
Wrappers, tins and bottle tops
Have a go, it's not a show.
Do not be a joke
Be good folk!

Jade Paterson (10)
Cockton Hill Junior School, Bishop Auckland

How To Save The Trees

Trees are friendly, happy and kind
You will never know it
Until you try talking to them
Don't be nasty, they can hear you know
They won't like it
If you say nasty things to them
Save the paper
Use the back
Recycle the paper
The trees will be back.

Laura Eales (9)
Cockton Hill Junior School, Bishop Auckland

Trees

Stop chopping down trees for paper
Just use recycled paper
Trees help our environment look nice
Animals live in trees, you can chop them down with them in
Don't chop down trees just for wood for us
Use the ones that are already chopped down.

Sara Winter (10)
Cockton Hill Junior School, Bishop Auckland

Litter Rap

Don't drop litter
It'll make you fitter.

Walk to the bin
And put your rubbish in.

Rubbish is mean
Keep our environment clean.

The world needs to be seen
So keep it green.

Megan Kennedy (10)
Cockton Hill Junior School, Bishop Auckland

The Deadly War

When I hear about the war
It feels as though I've hit a door.

The war is so bad
It makes everyone feel sad.

All those people get killed
And all those things they have to build.

The war is so crazy
It hurts my mate called Daisy.

All those guns make pollution
They have no solution.

Put a stop to this now
But we've got to think how.

Soldiers are dying
While the others are crying.

Nathan Dale (11)
Durham Lane Primary School, Eaglescliffe

Wars Are Wrong!

Wars are really bad,
If you saw one,
You'd be really sad.

Wars make people crazy,
Because in Iraq
You can't be lazy.

Wars should be out the door,
Because we don't want
Soldiers under our floor.

Zachary McAskill (11) & Ben Llewellyn (10)
Durham Lane Primary School, Eaglescliffe

Litter Is Shameful

L itter is shameful,
I t's disgraceful,
T he animals are dying,
T he climate is changing,
E very day is warmer,
R esult is litter.

I gnoring is dangerous,
S o stop and think,

S top this terrible torture,
H ate it the animals do,
A nimals suffer,
M ore die every day,
E co-friendly we could be,
F riendly to animals,
U nlike before,
L itter must stop!

Grace Brown (11) & Nina Marshall (10)
Durham Lane Primary School, Eaglescliffe

Be An Eco-Warrior

Eco-warrior, that's our name,
Saving the planet is our game,
We're not lying,
Our planet is dying,
So do something about it now
And we can make the world a better place.
How?

Pollution, disease,
You can, you can save it all,
We're not dim,
So recycle that tin,
Don't throw it in the bin.
Be an eco-warrior!

Megan Furr (11) & Emily McGuckin (10)
Durham Lane Primary School, Eaglescliffe

Save The Animals

The giant panda is an endangered animal
With their relative - the polar bear
These are both endangered bears
Do you want these animals to be extinct? Yeah?

A Javan rhino is really rare
People hunt these animals for their horns and hair
Another one is the black rhino
They might be extinct like the dinos.

Save these animals, save them now
Plant some trees to help their environment
Listen to what I'm saying
Otherwise your favourite animal will be dying!

Princedeep Randhawa & Hasnain Khan (11)
Durham Lane Primary School, Eaglescliffe

The Disease Poem

Find a disease,
Make it ease,
Have an injection,
Stop the infection.

If you've got a disease,
You will sneeze,
So beware,
Make sure you care.

Check out your disease
So people don't tease,
So don't start worrying
If people start bullying.

If you have a disease
It will spread with ease,
So stay inside
Then people don't hide.

Liam Davis (11) & Matthew Upson (10)
Durham Lane Primary School, Eaglescliffe

Be An Eco Friend

Be an eco friend to rainforests, animals and plants.
Don't let people destroy our plants, animals and rainforests
 with pollution and litter.
All you have to do is recycle a can every day and walk to school.
It will make a great difference,
Come on eco friends, we can, we can save the world.
All you've got to do is join us in our march to save the world
And all these poor animals, animals that are being terrorised
 by Man's killing machines
So come on eco friends, we can save the world.
Don't let litter get in our way, say no to pollution.
Come on eco friends, we can do it,
Do what's right and save the world.
Come on eco friends!

Patrick Carroll & Graham Dodds (10)
Durham Lane Primary School, Eaglescliffe

Mad Litter

When I see litter
It makes my mouth go bitter
It's all over the world
It's just blatantly hurled into the sea
Boy it makes me mad.

Every day is Earth Day
If it's cold or wet or hot
Pitch in to help save the planet
It's the only one we've got
So let's help save our planet
So here's an idea
Do your bit for the 'big green challenge'
Yeah!

Bailey Peacock Farrell & Alex Close (11)
Durham Lane Primary School, Eaglescliffe

Drip Drop!

Drip drop,
Won't it stop?
Time flies by,
It's not a lie,
Drip drop.

Never waiting,
Forever hating,
The way it never ends.

Won't it stop?
Drip drop.

You can make it drip drop,
Or you can make it *stop!*

Like teardrops it falls,
Silently it calls.

But no one ever notices,

Won't it stop?
Drip drop.

You can make it drip drop,
Or you can make it *stop!*

Turn the tap off,
Make it stop!
You can make it drip drop,
Or you can make it *stop!*

Antonia Phillips, Annabelle Lamond & Shauna McGahan (11)
Durham Lane Primary School, Eaglescliffe

The Climate Change

From Antarctica to Africa
From cold to hot
Now what a shock
The climate change.

Polar bears dying
Tigers crying
Because of the climate change
Now what a shame, the climate change.

From country to country
The weather is a change
Animals are beginning to faint
Oh no, the climate change.

Holly Chapman & Lauren Speight (11)
Durham Lane Primary School, Eaglescliffe

Freedom For Life

Recycle for our lives,
Recycle for our country,
Now recycle everyone
And give up deadly poverty.

Children's lives in danger,
That's poverty alright,
Think about them someday,
Think with all your might.

Racism is deadly,
Racism can kill,
It's your worst nightmare
And it'll be on your bill.

It's time to be free for life
And now it's true and clear,
That recycling is what we need
But the end is near.

Amyleigh Stewart & Robyn Watler (11)
Percy Main Primary School, North Shields

Our World

I remember my grandad telling me the world as it was yesterday
And then I remember him telling me as it is today.

The ozone layer's been destroyed
And the forests are disappearing,
Factories are growing larger,
We're slowly destroying the Earth.

We're all starting wars,
Not just against each other,
We're hunting down endangered animals
And making them extinct.

Car fumes are killing many things,
Such as the ozone layer
And in a hundred years or so
The sun could burn our soul.

What can we do to help our fragile world?

Thomas Hand (11)
Seaburn Dene Primary School, Sunderland

Think

Think about a world without any animals
Why are we cutting and chopping?
Would we like it if our homes were destroyed?
Think and stop it.

Think about a world without trees
Why are we not recycling?
Don't bin, recycle!
Think and stop it.

Think about a world of war
Is that what you want?
No, so think and *stop!*

Rebecca Hargate (11)
Seaburn Dene Primary School, Sunderland

What Is Going To Happen?

What is going to happen?

Nobody cares about the world
As it is slowly dying off.
Car fumes puff for every mile
But no one cares to walk,
Though walking is healthier,
Driving is easier.
Everyone should respect the environment
And cycle or walk.

What is going to happen?

Everyone should try to walk,
Or maybe even cycle.
But everyone decides to drive
And pollute the air around us.
But what will happen if we don't walk or cycle?
While we are driving in our cars
We don't realise we are killing the Earth slowly.

Dominic Shepherd (11)
Seaburn Dene Primary School, Sunderland

Think Of A World

Think of a world without any violence
Think of a world without any food.

Think of a world without any litter
Think of a world without any war.

Think of a world full of animals
They will be all gone very soon.

Think of a world with a lot of recycling
It would make the world a better place.

Do you like this world?

Denys Gardner (11)
Seaburn Dene Primary School, Sunderland

Disasters And Extinction

In some parts of the world
Many people wake up
Without a home beside them
Without food when they need it
Without shelter when they need it
Our world, the rubbish bin.

The rainforests are an Aladdin's Cave
Disappearing at an alarming rate
This makes me feel so angry
The creatures who once lived are forgotten
People in the world, they are crazy
To destroy such a tranquil place.

Daniel Atchison (11)
Seaburn Dene Primary School, Sunderland

War

Wars are pointless
Wars are today
What can we do with this world
When World War III is on the way?

People are starving
People are praying
People are angry
People are fading.

The world is dying
The world is polluted
The world is lost
The world is no more.

Stop the fighting now
Give us some peace in the world
The world is nearly over.

Tom Whiffen (11)
Seaburn Dene Primary School, Sunderland

What Litter Is Doing To The World

Litter is all over the planet
What is going to happen to the Earth?
Why can't people just put rubbish in the bin?
Lots of public places are drowned by rubbish!
People cannot have fun on the beach,
Children cannot take their shoes off.
Can you help?
Why can't people *stop* putting chewing gum on the pavement?
Can you help?

Lillie Keeling (10)
Seaburn Dene Primary School, Sunderland

We're All Destroying The World

Destruction! Homes, environment, animals,
We're all destroying the world.

Pollution! Rivers, air, animals, humans,
We're all destroying the world.

Racism! Splitting the world in two,
We're all destroying the world.

Think of a world without food,
Think of a world without plants,
Think of a world without animals,
Think of a world without humans.

Think, we're destroying the world.

Think of a world where we all share,
Think of a world where we're all kind,
Think of a world where there's no pollution,
Think of a world with no war.

Do you want a world like this?

Sam Johnson (10)
Seaburn Dene Primary School, Sunderland

The World Is Dying!

I look around,
The sun shone,
The world is dying.
Where have the rainforests gone?

I look around,
I can't stand it anymore,
The world is dying.
Why are there wars?

I look around,
There are people outside,
The world is dying.
Where have their homes gone?

I look around,
I am thrown to the ground,
The world is dying.
I see different diseases as I look around.

I look around,
There is rubbish everywhere,
The world is dying.
Why are people littering?

We have to save the world
Because the world is dying!

Jack Teasdale (11)
Seaburn Dene Primary School, Sunderland

What Have We Done?

How can we all change?
Crisp wrappers, sweet wrappers
Lying on the floor.
Lollipops, make-up
Blowing all about.
What have we done?

People flinging, people throwing
Half the world has disappeared.
Behind the trees, under bushes,
People don't even care.
What have we done?

The world is crying, the world is dying
All because of us.
Half the world has disappeared.
Where has it gone?
What have we done?

We could all try and change
To try and save our world.
We should clean up our world
Until we see the world again.
It's finally clean.
Hooray!

Carla Topliff (11)
Seaburn Dene Primary School, Sunderland

Why Can't We Change?

Why can't we change?

The world is dying slowly,
Trees get the chop!
All these gases and fumes,
Killing off the crops.

Why can't we change?

The Earth is covered in pollution,
Coke cans, the whole lot!
Oil spillages cover the beach
And mouldy yoghurt pots.

Why can't we change?

No one works together,
They do things against the law,
Racism and swearing,
They may even start a war!

Why can't we change?

We're not being fair to the world,
Spoiling its 'Aladdin's Cave' and treasures,
All this destruction is our fault
And we must change!

Now I've finished off my poem,
But these things still go on,
Only we can make them *stop!*
So work together and help, *come on!*

Rebecca Louise Ridley (11)
Seaburn Dene Primary School, Sunderland

What Have We Done?

The rainforest, so thick and bright,
Used to be so wonderful,
But now it is dead and gone,
How can we put things right?
What have we done?

The rivers and lakes were brimming with light,
Now they are brown and dark,
No light whatsoever,
I've trFied to change with all my might!
What have we done?

What about the ozone?
It is still in the sky,
It sits there large and now thin
It sits invisible to the eye.
What have we done?

How about poverty?
Children small and thin,
How can we help them?
How can we help them win?
What have we done?

So now I have finished my poem,
But all of this continues,
So try to do the best you can,
The world we cannot lose!
What can we do?

Jessica Green (11)
Seaburn Dene Primary School, Sunderland

What Will Happen To The World?

Day after day a steel beast eats into the rainforest,
Day after day unknown species of plants are thrown away,
Day after day lots of animals are carelessly killed.
What will happen to the world?

Day after day lorries pour endless rubbish into landfills,
Day after day recyclable materials are thrown away,
Day after day tonnes of litter is thrown away on the ground.
What will happen to the world?

Day after day people continue as normal with diseases,
Day after day people go to rivers to get dirty water,
Day after day people start with not much to eat.
What will happen to the world?

Haydn Evans (11)
Seaburn Dene Primary School, Sunderland

Animals And Extinction

Animals are amazing,
However dying every day,
Extinction is coming closer,
Their populations are moving away.

Habitats are being lost,
Destroyed in every way,
Extinction is coming closer,
Their populations are moving away.

Rhinos and orang-utans,
Sea lions making waves,
Extinction is coming closer,
Their populations are moving away.

Man is the biggest hunter,
Slaughtering every day,
Extinction is here now,
Their populations have moved away.

James Robson (11)
Seaburn Dene Primary School, Sunderland

What Have We Done To The World?

What have we done to the world?
With the overspilling landfills
And empty crisp packets flying in the air.
What have we done to the world?

What have we done to the world?
With cars spewing petrol into the atmosphere
And treacherous factories pumping out damaging gasses.
What have we done to the world?

What have we done to the world?
With those monstrous bulldozers,
Killing our precious rainforests.
What have we done to the world?

What have we done to the world?

Adam Coombs (11)
Seaburn Dene Primary School, Sunderland

What Have We Done?

What have we done to the plants
That once stood tall and proud?
We need to change our killing ways.
I've tried to speak out loud.

What have we done to the animals
That lived many years ago?
Soon they will all be extinct
A bit like the dodo.

What is the point in poverty,
Children so small and thin?
How can we give them what they want?
How can we help them win?

So now I have proved my point to you
About all that's going on,
If our ways are not changed
Soon it will be all gone.

Mae Heskett (10)
Seaburn Dene Primary School, Sunderland

Where Are The Animals?

Where are the plants?
Where are the colours?
And most importantly, where are the animals?

Where is the joy?
Where is the laughter?
And most importantly, where are the animals?

Where are the hippos?
Where are the rhinos?
And most importantly, where are the animals?

Where is the earth?
Where is the wood?
And most importantly, where are the animals?

I am all alone now waiting to go
But first I want you to know how we all go.

Without the trees,
Without the leaves,
What have we to eat?

Without the grass,
Without the Earth
Where have we to stand?

Philip Jones (11)
Seaburn Dene Primary School, Sunderland

What Is There?

What is there?
A polar bear.
But for how much longer?
The ice is melting.

What is there?
A monkey.
But for how much longer?
The trees are going, going, going.
No more swinging, no more fun.

What is there?
A dolphin.
But for how much longer?
Pollution is here, oh my, oh dear.

What is there?
An elephant.
But for how much longer?
They've been on the Earth for 39 million years
And might be gone in 10 years.

What has gone?
The dodo.
It's been gone for years.
Humans did it, it's our fault!

Do something!

Amy Lamming (11)
Seaburn Dene Primary School, Sunderland

What's The Matter With That?

Piano keys are black and white,
They work together,
Why can't we be like that?

TVs used to be black and white,
We lived with it,
Why can't we be like that?

Black and white go together,
On a football strip perhaps,
Why can't we be like that?

But people, mmm . . .
Don't work together,
What's the matter with that?

Everything!

Shelley Nicholson (11)
Seaburn Dene Primary School, Sunderland

The World

The world on this day
Needs to recycle,
The rubbish about
Is causing pollution,
The air's filled with gas,
You can't see far,
But you can help,
So clean up your rubbish.

The world on this day
Is not very peaceful,
People carry knives,
It's not very safe
To walk on the streets,
We can help,
So take more care.

David Parnaby (10)
Seaburn Dene Primary School, Sunderland

Homeless

What is the cause of homelessness?
What is the cause of loneliness?
What happened to you and me?
Walking on the street.
Wind around my feet.
I am homeless.

When will I have my next meal?
What will happen next to me?
As I walk back to my street.
The wind around my feet.
I am homeless.

When will I be helped?
The rain falling to the ground
And the streets are silent.
As I sit on my street.
Wind at my feet.
I am homeless.

Molly Mae Lloyd (11)
Seaburn Dene Primary School, Sunderland

Rainforests

I am a tree
Big and tall,
As you see,
There are trees,
All over the world,
Stood up straight
Or even curled.

People chop, slice
And even tear,
But in the end,
There's no home for a bear.

Lauren Brough (11)
Seaton Sluice County Middle School, Whitley Bay

A Dark Day

The sun is not glowing
It's not just the clouds that are in the way
The wind is blowing
It's a dark day
Factories are huffing and puffing
The air is choking
Smoke has covered everything
No one can see
Trees are being cut down in their prime
Animals are dying
We're wasting our time
It's a dark day
A blast from the past has ruined our future
Let's stop this madness now
Rhinos and elephants are going to be extinct
Do you have the heart to care?
The sun is not glowing
It's not just the clouds that are in the way
The wind is blowing
It is a dark day.

Katie Pearson (10)
Seaton Sluice County Middle School, Whitley Bay

Home

Tigers, monkeys in the zoo,
Deer, pandas and lions too,
While baby animals live alone
And other animals have a home,
Squirrels on the trees they roam,
But soon they have no home,
Animals dead, shot in the head,
They would live if they had a home,
So they would not be cold and live alone.

Rachel Davison (11)
Seaton Sluice County Middle School, Whitley Bay

Extinction

Tigers, chimps and lions too,
You'll only see these animals in the zoo.
The ice caps are melting down, down low,
The polar bears are sheltering in the snow.
Soon the snow will be all gone,
Because the sun has brightly shone.

The greedy farmers rip up the shoots
Whilst all the trees lose their roots.
The farmers don't realise what they're doing
To the Earth itself and the damage they're producing.
We have to stop now and help this planet,
Before it's too late and we can't.

Jessica McCafferty (11)
Seaton Sluice County Middle School, Whitley Bay

Extinction

The extinction of animals is really bad,
I start to wonder, it makes me sad,
They're walking around in an unknown place,
You should see the pity on their face,
Animals' lives are fastly sinking,
I worry what their minds are thinking,
We've seen dogs and cats in alleyways
But it's lions and tigers I like today.
So now you know what extinction's like
It's giving me a bit of a fright,
But at least now the truth is out,
We know that animals wander about.

Steven Doris (11)
Seaton Sluice County Middle School, Whitley Bay

Global Warming

The streets are smelly and very unclean,
We need your help to make the world green,
So pick up some litter and stop being bitter
Or we'll end up in the gutter.

Your car needs to stop,
Or the animals will drop,
Precious things will be erased
And never replaced,
Give Mother Nature a break for heaven's sake,
'Cause after all we're killing us all.

We need to stop it now
So the temperature doesn't rise,
People, plants and animals will die.

If global warming happens
It will not be good for our Earth and neighbourhood,
It will make the world hot,
Just like a boiling pot.

If global warming affects the Earth,
Then Mother Nature could not give birth.

What are we?
We are killers, killing the Earth.

What are we?
We are polluters, polluting the Earth.

What are we?
We are destroying Mother Nature.
We need to act now
And life might not end if you're the Earth's friend.

Aimee Pearson (10)
Seaton Sluice County Middle School, Whitley Bay

War

People start wars who want to kill,
Just for the thrill.
They kill for land, lots of land and countries.
Soldiers kill each other,
With nuclear weapons that cause mass destruction.
They should be destroyed,
Soldiers, planes and all sorts of vehicles blow up each other.
Men want to kill each other with anything they can get hold of.
War, can we stop it now before it wipes out mankind,
Off the face of the Earth.
Help, help!

Ayrton Browning (11)
Seaton Sluice County Middle School, Whitley Bay

Disease

Disease is attacking,
So you better get packing,
Pain is unfair,
It causes you despair.
Famine is spreading like butter on bread,
Be careful or you'll be dead.
Death is near,
This is no time to be drinking beer.
Dead bodies in the water,
Disease loves to slaughter.
You beg for mercy,
There's no one left in the nursery!

Joseph Woods (10)
Seaton Sluice County Middle School, Whitley Bay

Pollution

P lease help our environment,
O ur world is stuck and needs help,
L et's all do it together,
L ove and care for the environment,
U se helpful advice,
T alk to someone,
I n school, a teacher, helper or friend,
O r go on the Internet,
N ot enough people are helping,
   so will you?

Jasmine Common (10)
Seaton Sluice County Middle School, Whitley Bay

Pollution

Animals all staring,
At the monstrous machines,
The whistle starts blowing
And out comes the steam.

Trees starting falling,
Animals start scrambling,
For the freedom they need,
All because of the humans' greed.

Pollution is very wrong
And it gives out quite a pong,
So we need to do something about it now,
We need help to clean up this messy ground.

Amber Wakenshaw (11)
Seaton Sluice County Middle School, Whitley Bay

Homeless

Got no home, got no money.
Having no food is not so funny.
Little fires just to keep warm.
When they should have a nice cosy home.
Sleeping on the floor every night.
Just gives them a bit of a fright.
We're so lucky, we're so rich.
We're not the ones sleeping in a ditch.
So please give a thought
To all those that are homeless
That aren't so fortunate as you and me.

Lewis Devlin (10)
Seaton Sluice County Middle School, Whitley Bay

Save The Rainforest

The rainforest is never quiet,
The rainforest is always loud,
To hear the teeth-chattering roar of the tiger,
But that is not the case anymore,
You barely hear the relaxing sound of the grasshopper's song,
Or the sloths as they haul themselves along,
You rarely hear the tiger's call, the greatest hunter of them all,
Prowling silently to reach his prey,
Guzzling, feeding every day,
Trees are disappearing at an astonishing rate,
Just so we can fill our plate,
All this life and beauty gone,
But Man's ignorance still goes on.

Laura Davies (9)
Seaton Sluice County Middle School, Whitley Bay

The Tiger

The tiger stalked,
Silent and scared,
As she wearily walked,
But then stopped and stared.
Her home was gone,
Her cubs lost too,
The scalding sun shone,
As she trudged on through.
The destroyed remains,
Of the forest, once green
Now monstrous cranes,
Were all that could be seen.
She's on worn out feet,
The lakes are all dry,
There's nothing to eat,
Soon she could die.
It's going to be tough,
For her to survive,
Her life will be rough,
If she wants to stay alive.

Charlotte Harris (11)
Seaton Sluice County Middle School, Whitley Bay

Rainforest

R ainforest dying, alarming rate,
A nimals crying of extinction,
I n the forest they may roam,
N ight and day they will groan,
F rom starvation can they suffer?
O range tigers are not much tougher,
R ough the stones they will get,
E very day, step by step,
S trolling along the dusty path,
T ill they stop and say,
   'Save the rainforest today!'

Sophie Brownlee (10)
Seaton Sluice County Middle School, Whitley Bay

Protect The Animal Kingdom

Animals are disappearing really fast,
The ones that are left are now the last,
But don't give up hope
And don't be a dope,
We can still save them,
Just by doing a simple thing,
Like throwing our rubbish in the bin.
You'll be sorry, so don't let them slip out of the world,
Save the animals for all that's good.
Please, help them!

Evan Johnson (10)
Seaton Sluice County Middle School, Whitley Bay

Rainforest Rescue

Save the rainforest and the creatures in it,
Let tigers live and all the other amazing things,
Let them live and breed,
Those land developers are full of greed,
Stop extinction,
Let bugs, bears and chimps live,
Don't kill them or make them limp,
And all the landslides,
Might as well be a country to capsize!
So help the rainforest
And make us proud,
Don't make it bad like a big black cloud,
So come on and help us all,
And all those trees that stand so tall.

Liam Carroll (10)
Seaton Sluice County Middle School, Whitley Bay

In The Jungle
(Inspired by song 'The Lion Sleeps Tonight' South African Zulu folk song)

In the jungle,
The mighty jungle
The lumberjacks cut the trees.

In the jungle,
The mighty jungle
Poachers killing the animals.

A wimoweh, a wimoweh,
A wimoweh, a wimoweh.

In the jungle,
The mighty jungle
The birds are falling out of the sky.

Carl Howes (11)
Seaton Sluice County Middle School, Whitley Bay

Homelessness

No house, no home,
No place to belong,
No food, no drink,
Not even a bone.

A life of misery,
A life of pain,
A single mutt as my only mate.

No money, no nothing,
No room for a bed,
This lil' old man, almost dead.

Ryan Armiger (11)
Seaton Sluice County Middle School, Whitley Bay

Stop And Think!

The Earth used to be a fascinating place,
Now the Earth is a disgrace,
People starving on the streets,
No bed covered in sheets,
Dogs will yelp,
Tigers will prowl,
Thinking the world is foul,
No hunting for the bears,
They will think no one cares,
Save the world, give us hope,
This world really can't cope!

Olivia Jarvis (10)
Seaton Sluice County Middle School, Whitley Bay

Guess Who?

I pollute,
I kill,
I make animals ill,
I float through the air,
But I don't care,
The only clue I give you
Is indeed my stench,
I float past you
And feel your heart wrench.

Who am I?
Answer: Pollution.

Darcey Hannah Falconer (9)
Seaton Sluice County Middle School, Whitley Bay

Endangered Animals

Endangered animals all around,
Endangered animals drop dead on Earth's ground,
Wild ass, tigers and deer,
Hope this helps make everything clear,
Vivisection is also wrong,
It's been going on for far too long,
Crazy scientists test on them,
I know it's to help us but erm . . .
I do not know what else to say,
But I hope you help make a difference one day.

Lauren Devlin (11)
Seaton Sluice County Middle School, Whitley Bay

Rainforest

The enormous big rainforest,
Standing large and proud,
Along comes the cutter which is very loud,
The animals flee with terror,
And then the animals become extinct,
That really stinks,
I hope this poem changes your mind
Because cutting down trees
Is really unkind.

Charlie Turney (11)
Seaton Sluice County Middle School, Whitley Bay

Recycle, Reuse, Reduce The Waste We Use

Stop next time you buy wood
Because lush green forest gets chopped down
As animals get extinct and lose their homes
It does not help if we leave rubbish on the ground
So animals get trapped in our rubbish and die
Recycle, reuse, reduce the waste we use
Because everything we recycle, reuse, reduce
Is one more step to save the Earth
So next time think before you bin.

Emma Bentley (11)
Seaton Sluice County Middle School, Whitley Bay

The World

Pollution floating in the air,
Animals dying everywhere,
Cut down on cars and factory smoke,
Sponsor an animal then there's hope,
Litter blowing in the breeze,
Friendly people catching disease,
Everyone please pick up your mess,
Healthy people less and less,
Rainforests getting cut down,
Racism wandering round the town,
Don't throw magazines away, re-read,
Don't be scared and you'll succeed.

Lucy Thompson (11)
Seaton Sluice County Middle School, Whitley Bay

Racism

It doesn't matter if you're black or white,
No one needs to have a fight,
It doesn't matter if you speak English or not,
Everyone was a baby in a cot,
Everyone is the same under our skin,
Everyone should have a chance of being a king.

Chloe Tweedy (10)
Seaton Sluice County Middle School, Whitley Bay

The Tree And Swan

I live in the rainforest,
I'm a tree in fact.
But I'm in a lot of pain
Because I'm dying of acid rain.
The massive machines tore apart my family
And now are after me.

I live in the rivers and streams,
I'm a swan in fact.
My home is being polluted
And feathers are not white but black.
Me and my family are still intact
But soon we'll be going to a new habitat.

Kate Foster (11)
Seaton Sluice County Middle School, Whitley Bay

Animals

Chipmunks, squirrels, cobra snakes,
Including fish from their lakes.
For these animals have to hide,
The hunters are coming.
Rats, bats, cats, wombats,
Jumping from tree to tree.
For these animals have to hide,
The hunters are coming.
All these animals jumping for joy,
This includes orang-utans,
For these animals are free,
The hunters are gone!

Daniel McDougal (11)
Seaton Sluice County Middle School, Whitley Bay

Litter

Litter is untidy,
Litter is a mess,
It makes me angry,
So I have to stress,
People scatter it around,
All over the ground,
We all try to stop it,
But people carry on,
Please stop littering,
Around the ground,
Then we will have a cleaner world.

Christina Kelly (11)
Seaton Sluice County Middle School, Whitley Bay

Save The World

Don't drop litter
It is so bitter
Recycling makes the world bloom
If you drop litter it will go *boom!*
Help the world save most of the rainforest
Without trees we will die
I don't want to die
Do you want your children to die?
So you recycle and that won't happen
If you raise money to keep the trees
The world won't die soon
You can stop this if you grow your own trees
I'm sure you don't want to die
Think of our lovely world.

Zoe Fox (10)
Seaton Sluice County Middle School, Whitley Bay

Save Our World

S ave our world
A ll animals must be saved
V andalism must be stopped
E veryone must stop using cars

O ur world is a disgrace
U ntil we stop using cars the air will be polluted
R oads are busy now, day in and day out

W ould our world ever change?
O ur world smells
R ubbish put in the bins
L ive in a better place while you can
D iesel is much better than petrol.

Carl Larmouth (10)
Seaton Sluice County Middle School, Whitley Bay

Save Our World

S ave our planet
A nd we will exist.
V ictory will be ours if we listen to others.
E ngland will help.

O ceans will not flood all over the world.
U nless we save the world we will not exist.
R educe, recycle, reuse and we will save the world.

W e will save the world.
O ur people will save energy if we
R educe, recycle, reuse.
L earn more about reduce, recycle, reuse.
D on't do it too late, recycle today.

David Homer (10)
Seaton Sluice County Middle School, Whitley Bay

The Green Machine

Recycling is the best
Now put it to the test,
Put your cans in a recycling bin
To make a light work for 3 hours,
Recycle paper and plastic
In the recycling bin,
Be nice to your planet
And help it to recycle.

Jenny Marshall (10)
Seaton Sluice County Middle School, Whitley Bay

E Is For Endangered

A is for Asian elephant, deforestation is its threat to survival.
B is for blue whale, the hunter is its enemy.
C is for chimpanzee, habitat destruction will wipe it out.
G is for giant panda, extraordinarily rare and legally protected
                                                     from poachers.
H is for Hawaiian monk seal, there are less than 1000 left in the wild.
J is for jaguar, a beautifully spotted cat but to the farmer a nuisance.
R is for red wolf, nearly extinct because of human growth.
T is for Tasmanian forester kangaroo hunted for its meat.
L is for *let them live*.

Robert Lydon (10)
Seaton Sluice County Middle School, Whitley Bay

The World

Recycle, recycle the world is sad,
So we don't have to be bad,
We have to clean up like mad.
Glass bottles in special bins,
So we can make more and more things.
Plastic tubs, cardboard and paper,
We put in different bins to help out nature.
Pollution, pollution is getting worse,
We have to try and put it in reverse.
By cutting down on fuel and carbon gases,
This helps pollution by masses.

Harry Pearson (10)
Seaton Sluice County Middle School, Whitley Bay

Poem Mix

The more pollution the less world there is to live on,
So please stop polluting or there won't be anyone left to stop it.
If we keep on polluting the world,
More animals will be extinct,
They will die because they will have no food left.
We shouldn't use cars that often
Because the petrol is bad for the environment.
We need to recycle more,
We should send our toys and clothes away
So that other people can use them.
Help the world to help yourself.

Michael John Maley (10)
Seaton Sluice County Middle School, Whitley Bay

Danger!

Danger! Danger!
The animals are in danger,
Can we help them?
Then how do we help them?
Do not litter,
You could kill them all.
Recycle wood
So you can see the wonders of the woods.

Callum Martin (9)
Seaton Sluice County Middle School, Whitley Bay

Litter

Litter, litter everywhere,
All the horrible people don't care,
Litter is a horrible sight,
All the loving people do care,
All the litter is killing all our creatures,
Why don't people care?

Dean Leon Hindmarch (9)
Seaton Sluice County Middle School, Whitley Bay

Untitled

Why litter when there's always a bin everywhere?
The cars are always polluting the air.
If you litter near a field a little hedgehog or rabbit
                        could get its nose stuck in a can.
What are you doing killing the environment?

Nathan Knight (10)
Seaton Sluice County Middle School, Whitley Bay

Save Our World!

If you stop pollution
This will be the solution,
If you stop global warming
We can stop the world, this is a warning!
Think green,
Keep it clean!
Stop global warming,
Make it a warning.
Think green,
Keep our Earth clean!
You may be harming.
Make a difference.

Jennifer Taylor (9)
Seaton Sluice County Middle School, Whitley Bay

War Is Bad

War! War! War!
It's very bad, it's very bad,
Litter! Litter! Litter!
It's on the ground and all around.
Recycling is good,
Littering is bad.
Let's save the world!

Thomas Bushell (10)
Seaton Sluice County Middle School, Whitley Bay

Wooden It Be Good?

Wood, wood everywhere,
But no tree in sight.
If this continues it could give the whole world a fright.
I know I have my wooden seat,
Where will the animals meet?
What will we breathe? What will we do
When all the rainforests are through?

Luke Whatmore (9)
Seaton Sluice County Middle School, Whitley Bay

Litter, Litter

Litter, litter everywhere
But nobody seems to care.
Plastic bags lying around
Why do they leave them on the ground?
People shouldn't be so mean
They should keep the streets clean.

James Cleghorn (10)
Seaton Sluice County Middle School, Whitley Bay

Pollution

Rubbish
Don't just fling it, bin it
Don't just bin it, look in it
Can you recycle it?
Then *do* it!

Adam Render (10)
Seaton Sluice County Middle School, Whitley Bay

Could Be Fun

Saving the world could be fun
If we just could get alone with each other.

Saving the world could be fun
If we could stop fighting each other.

Saving the world could be fun
If we looked after each other.

Saving the world could be fun
If we looked after our planet.

Stop the wars!
Stop being cruel!
Stop ignoring the problems!
Let the fun begin!

Jordan-Lee Hall (10)
Seaton Sluice County Middle School, Whitley Bay

War

War
It is happening all over the world,
People are dying,
Children are crying.
War
Men disagree, the guns come out,
Rockets are launched,
Attacks are made.
Where do people go?
Nowhere.
They have no homes, no food,
No life,
War.

Jamie McCafferty (10)
Seaton Sluice County Middle School, Whitley Bay

Climate Change

Climate change stops the world going round.
Its clouds of gas pulls the world down.
Factories and cars make the air thinner.
Continue like this and no one's a winner.
If the ice caps continue their slow demise
The oceans are continuously going to rise.
We need to use our heads and be a bit keener,
Make our world much, much greener.

Adam Duxfield (10)
Seaton Sluice County Middle School, Whitley Bay

Untitled

Make our world a better place
by using the big green poetry machine.
Stop the littering, stop the racism
and start recycling today.
All that climate change, pollution and extinction,
that is all because of us.
Come on, hurry up, save the day
and stop making a fuss.
Help other animals and people,
rainforests, plants and trees.
If you want to save the world
then why not start now.

Rachel Swarbrick (10)
Seaton Sluice County Middle School, Whitley Bay

Big Green Machine

B in it and box it
I nspire others to do the same.
G o green and help our planet.

G reen is fantastic, the more the better.
R aise money to help our rainforests.
E nvironmentally friendly.
E arth is sad.
N eed to keep our Earth safe.

M ake the Earth happy,
A ct now!
C hoose to walk to school.
H elp our animals.
I nstead of dropping litter pick it up.
N o more gasses.
E veryone must change.

Melissa Smith (10)
Seaton Sluice County Middle School, Whitley Bay

Stop Before You Chop!

Stop before you chop
Because rainforests get chopped down,
It is bad for our environment as well.
Many animals die because of us.
Stop before you bin,
Try this to save the Earth.
Recycle our rubbish,
Reduce the amount of rubbish we use.
Reuse the waste we use.

Amy Bentley (10)
Seaton Sluice County Middle School, Whitley Bay

The World Is Coming To An End

Litter and rubbish being thrown away,
That could be recycled from today,
The world is coming to an end!
Cars that pollute the beautiful sky,
Now the world is beginning to cry,
The world is coming to an end!
Fields and fields nearly gone
Houses and buildings built upon.
We need more trees
And flowers and the honeybees.
The world is coming to an end!

Sarah Bennett (11)
Seaton Sluice County Middle School, Whitley Bay

Litter

L ess wildlife
I nvisible nature
T errible happenings
T oo much trash
E victing people
R ubbish

So now you know
What is happening to this Earth,
Please help to make this planet a better place.

Rachael Burgess (9)
Seaton Sluice County Middle School, Whitley Bay

Soon Extinction Will Come

Soon extinction will come,
No creatures howling at the moon,
No room to keep a baboon,
Extinction will come soon,
While monkeys swing on trees,
Chasing lots of bees,
While we sit rattling our keys,
Extinction will come soon,
Racoons searching for food,
But they will not be in a good mood,
If all they have is gone!

Jessica Maley (10)
Seaton Sluice County Middle School, Whitley Bay

Our Planet Near Disaster

People on the streets,
Have no sheets,
They might freeze,
Don't please, please, please,
Things may poison my blood,
Like mud,
It needs to be dealt with,
Before the ice melts,
I demand,
For people to take command.

Chloe Miller (9)
Seaton Sluice County Middle School, Whitley Bay

Pollution

The Earth is a nice place,
Now pollution has got greater and greater,
It's a big disgrace,
Stop polluting the Earth.

Stop using cars,
Why don't you walk,
Stop using cars as much.

The North Pole is going to melt,
This is why it needs to be dealt with,
Stop polluting the Earth,
Stop cutting trees,
There's less oxygen,
Carbon dioxide's ring around the Earth,
Means heat going in but no cold getting out.

Tom James Ramsay (9)
Seaton Sluice County Middle School, Whitley Bay

Rainforests In Danger

We need your help to save the creatures,
To save all the rainforests' features,
All the plants will be extinct,
Why don't you stop and have a think,
The animals and people beg and hope,
So if you help they can cope,
Stop the companies that are cutting down trees,
So people that come and live here can see,
All the wonderful things that are here.

Robyn Connelly (10)
Seaton Sluice County Middle School, Whitley Bay

Animals' Extinction

Down in the rainforest
Animals live, roaring
Animals, slithering
Animals and others that exist.

But now the rainforest has gone
The animals, there are none.

That means no roaring lions
And no slithering snakes
They have been killed
Or put in the zoo.

I hear you asking
Where are the people?
I will give you a clue
They have died or are living in the houses
They might live near you.

Emma Doris (9)
Seaton Sluice County Middle School, Whitley Bay

Disease

D eadly and life spoiling,
I rritating and aggravating,
S addening,
E nding lives,
A ching,
S enseless,
E ndless.

Cameron Dunbar (10)
Seaton Sluice County Middle School, Whitley Bay

Homeless And Pollution

H ungry and helpless
O dorous
M en and women
E ducation lacking
L onely
E xiled
S quatters
S ad

P oisonous
'O rrible
L ung-harming
L ife-taking
U gly
T ainting
I nfectious
O iled
N asty.

Emily Clark (10)
Seaton Sluice County Middle School, Whitley Bay

The Homeless

People on the streets,
Living in cardboard boxes,
Keeping warm from a fire,
With no cosy beds,
They should be as lucky as us,
Help them by giving them food,
By donating money to them,
Then they will have a home,
Stop it or I will be sad
And eventually go mad.

Steven Simpson (10)
Seaton Sluice County Middle School, Whitley Bay

Endangered

Animals are galloping gracefully through rainforests,
Unusual but amazing,
Wonderful and magnificent,
However endangered!

Endangered by rainforest destruction,
Endangered by human hunting,
Endangered by successful, cunning plans.

We need to save animals from becoming extinct,
Let them live their lives,
Let the bees buzz in their hive,
Let the insects scuttle,
Let the monkeys chuckle.

Hear the lions roar,
It should be a law,
Let all animals live,
Treat animals as well as if they were humans,
They have as much a right to live as we do,
Save the animals!

Georgia Nunn (10)
Seaton Sluice County Middle School, Whitley Bay

Save The Animals

Animals are so beautiful,
From the tigers to the sloths,
We need to help save them from extinction,
You won't hear the tigers roar when they're all gone,
You won't see the sloths dangling on the branches,
Oh please, please, please,
Help us save the animals.

Kayleigh Wright (10)
Seaton Sluice County Middle School, Whitley Bay

Poverty And Disease In Africa

They haven't got money,
So they have to sleep on the street,
They get diseases that they can't beat,
They smell very foul,
But they haven't got a towel to wash with,
Factories puffing out pollution
And disruption on the streets,
What can you do?
We need your help
To save Africa!

Zoe Frances Martin (10)
Seaton Sluice County Middle School, Whitley Bay

What We Could Lose

Dolphins are smooth,
Horses have hooves,
If there is any race,
Tortoises will go at the slowest pace,
Tigers, no fins,
But leopards will win,
Dolphins are silky,
Cows are milky,
Leopards are spotty,
While a lion's mane can go knotty,
Lemurs are small with short hair,
Tigers trap their prey with a fierce glare.
If they were all gone, it would make me sad,
But also it would make me very mad.

Emily Stewart (9)
Seaton Sluice County Middle School, Whitley Bay

What Is The World Today?

What is the world today?
War, kills and murders,
Round every corner is death and destruction.
People helpless in the gloom,
Children in grief
And families in rage.
Bloodthirsty men with lethal weapons,
Killing anyone who gets their way.

What is the world today?
Animals are dying and it's all our fault,
We are destroying their home,
The beautiful rainforest.
Animals are fleeing from the destructive vehicles,
Most are nearly extinct.
We need to change!

Joseph Dungworth (11)
Seaton Sluice County Middle School, Whitley Bay

The Eco Way

Paper, cardboard and tins
Should all end up in the bins
Recycling is not hard to do
You just have to put it in the bin that's blue
Chewing gum stuck to my shoe
Drives me nuts, how about you?
Paper blowing in the air
What a mess everywhere!
Bins are there for a reason
You should use one every season.

Kelly Dawn Hilton (11)
Seaton Sluice County Middle School, Whitley Bay

Rainforests Need Help!

R ainforests are being cut down,
A nimals are getting hurt,
I n some rainforests there are barely any trees,
N ow some rainforests haven't got any trees!
F actories are taking trees for money,
O ther people are making room for crops,
R ainforests are special,
E veryone can help,
S ome of the trees are very tall,
T aller than 10 feet tall and are getting cut down
S ave the rainforests of the world!

Leonie Tia Stuart (10)
Seaton Sluice County Middle School, Whitley Bay

Extinction

Stop your people cutting down trees,
Because there's no place for bees,
And other animals becoming extinct,
Stop, stop and just think!
Beetles, frogs, snails, sloths, monkeys, birds and snakes
They're all becoming extinct.

If you cut down a tree,
It will leave you with a fee,
For this is the animals' home
And this is my poem.

Harry Green (11)
Seaton Sluice County Middle School, Whitley Bay

Recycling Is Now big In Our Town

Recycling is now big in our town,
Blue bins, green bins, bottle banks, all around.
We will stop the litter on the ground,
So please recycle and the world will change round,
So please help me recycle as much as we can,
Otherwise pollution will be cycling its way to our town.
Helpers are the people I thank,
So please everyone pick up the litter that's lurking all around,
So our town is clean and hygienic.

Blaise Charlton-Baird (10)
Seaton Sluice County Middle School, Whitley Bay

Animals In Extinction

Humans are killing Earth's animals
Tigers shot and skinned
Tusks from elephants ripped
Turtle eggs stolen to make people rich

Humans are killing Earth's animals
Cutting down animals' habitats
Polluting the waters with rubbish and poison
Capturing creatures to torture them for fun

How humans are helping Earth's animals
Banning and fining poachers
And donating to animal charities
You and I can help them

Animals are dying!
Animals are dying!
Animals are dying!
Help them before they're gone *forever!*

Sean Fulton (10)
Seaton Sluice County Middle School, Whitley Bay

Recycle It

This country is a mess!
Why is it a mess?
Some people just don't care
Dropping litter everywhere
Cardboard, cans to name but a few
This is what we need to do -
Plastic bottles will not rot in the ground
Let us use them again - pass them around
Reuse and recycle is the name of the game
To spoil planet Earth would be such a *shame!*

Kyle Hall (11)
Seaton Sluice County Middle School, Whitley Bay

Bitter Litter

Pandas are dying -
I'm not lying
We're cutting down too many trees
Leave the trees alone!

Litter everywhere
I think it is wrong to treat our environment like this
Pick it up and put it in a bin

If we all work together
I'm sure we'll find a cure
To save our animals
And keep our world safe and tidy.

Jessica Govan
Seaton Sluice County Middle School, Whitley Bay

Rainforest

Rainforests have lost more than half of their trees in the last 50 years.
The Amazon rainforest is at most risk.
Rainforests have 5 layers, the bottom layer is called the ground layer
And the top layer is called the emergent layer.
Damaging rainforests can damage the world in many other ways.
Most rainforests need a climate that is hot and cold.
There should be many hours of sunshine in rainforests.
Different types of species of plant and animals live in the
 tropical rainforests
And the population in the rainforest is growing very, very fast.
Many people live in the rainforest and need the trees to live.
People have cleared huge areas of the rainforest in South America,
So *please stop!*

Bridie Nicole Knights (10)
Seaton Sluice County Middle School, Whitley Bay

Extinction

How sad the beauty of Mother Earth
Our children will never see
Extinction all because of greed
They want to see the creatures
I can't imagine Mother Earth without God's creatures wild
Protect them now for us today and for tomorrow's child
And somewhere in the oceans deep
Somewhere in woodlands dense
To never know a bullet's pain
Or be held back by a fence
See your animals fade away
Because they won't be the very next day
That is the price we have to pay.

Scott Carlisle (10)
Seaton Sluice County Middle School, Whitley Bay

Pollution And The Homeless

A tear from the eye, a child on the street.
Hugging her mother tight.
Being homeless isn't funny.
It's just sad.
They light up to keep warm,
But they have no home to go in, no family to keep safe.
Kicking cans up and down the street is all they can do
                                                       to keep awake.
Tiny children cry and wail from starvation.
Their mothers try to keep them warm.
Poor children, nothing to do unlike us.
Hunting for food along back alleys,
Drinking from puddles, all dirty and muddy
And worst of all having a bath if they're lucky.

Jessica Nicole Wood (10)
Seaton Sluice County Middle School, Whitley Bay

Extinction

There are many animals in the wild
I've seen many that are very riled
Most are endangered
And some are being led to extinction
Due to log companies
Who are adding pollution to all the countries
But you can help to save the plants!
The creatures and the people of the *rainforest!*

Tammi Berresford (9)
Seaton Sluice County Middle School, Whitley Bay

Littering

When you drop your litter
On the ground,
You're littering up our world,
With glass bottles, chewing gum and paper.
Animals can be harmed,
If treading on the glass,
Shoes can be ruined,
With chewing gum.
No wonder our towns and cities
Are beginning to look glum,
Put your rubbish in a bin,
Littering is such a sin.

Jennifer Drake-Browning (11)
Seaton Sluice County Middle School, Whitley Bay

Being Homeless

B eing homeless is not fun.
E ndless nights on the streets.
I ll with my very, very, very unhappy life.
N asty chemicals on the pavement.
G arbage is everywhere.

H omeless is without a home.
O verlooked and alone.
M ice scatter around us.
E very day is the same.
L itter swirls around
E verywhere.
S uffering is here.
S adness too.

Alannah Willis Harvey (11)
Seaton Sluice County Middle School, Whitley Bay

Don't Drop It, Bin It

L itter, litter everywhere, making such a mess
I f only others cared as much and recycled their litter
T reat the world with respect
T idy away leaving lovely streets
E ncourage everyone to recycle and reuse
R emember, we only have one world, *so please look after it . . .*

Jane Roberts (10)
Seaton Sluice County Middle School, Whitley Bay

Save The Earth That We Now Stand!

Litter is rolling on the ground,
Pollution is flowing all around
And if we don't do something soon,
I'm willing to blast to the moon.
Put all the litter in the bin,
Environmentally friendly cars have the big win!
Start recycling for the harmless trees,
Plant some plants for the honey bees
And since we only have one world,
Look after the world on my word.
We need oxygen to survive,
So we need more trees to arrive!
The ozone layer is going quick,
So the polar bears are at risk.
If we can't stop it soon,
The human population might die out,
So listen to the words I shout,
So we can do what's right for us
And so we don't turn to crust!

Shannon Little (10)
Seaton Sluice County Middle School, Whitley Bay

Bottles

Don't drop any bottles - because they clatter
Open a bottle of wine and watch it shatter.
Don't just stand and watch it break
Take it to the bottle bank for goodness sake!
When you've finished drinking your pop -
Return your bottle to the shop!
We need to stop this senseless littering
Before our world is garbage!

Chantelle Lucas (10)
Seaton Sluice County Middle School, Whitley Bay

Change Our World

L ousy litter cluttering our streets.
I f only everyone cared as much.
T he streets would be a nicer place to be.
T idy, sweep, bag and bin it.
E ncourage all to respect their world.
R emove, clean and recycle your rubbish
   to help change our world . . .

Christopher Kennedy (11)
Seaton Sluice County Middle School, Whitley Bay

Litter

Litter is bad.
Litter is as useful as a broken motorbike.
Why stand and drop it?
Put it in a bin!
Or . . .
Reuse!
Reduce!
Recycle!
Use the 3Rs!

Marcus Matthewson (11)
Seaton Sluice County Middle School, Whitley Bay

The Truth

More and more animals becoming extinct,
Along with the rainforest they used to be linked,
Animals losing their habitat,
But I have more to say about that,
The animals were great in the past,
If we don't change our ways they will never last.

Lauren Hindmarch (11)
Seaton Sluice County Middle School, Whitley Bay

Rain

Rain, rain clatter on the roof,
Rain, rain it really matters,
How would you use it?
Can be very useful.
Rain, rain - use it very carefully,
It always matters.

*I am doing it for my mum
And on behalf of St Oswald's Hospice.
They looked after my mam.
Unfortunately she died when I was 8 years old
On 20th November 2004.*

Daniel James Meredith (11)
Seaton Sluice County Middle School, Whitley Bay

Affecting The World

One piece of litter could change the world,
So don't leave it lying on pavements
Or the world might change once again.

Graffiti there and in alleyways
Don't let the chavs make a mess
Or the world might change once again.

Paul O'Malley (11)
The Avenue Primary School, Nunthorpe

Recycling!

Crush your bottles with your hands,
Crush you cans with your feet,
Crush your bottles with your hands,
Crush your cans with your feet,
To keep the world looking neat.

Your garden waste is messing up the place,
Cardboard everywhere a big disgrace,
Your garden waste is messing up the place,
Cardboard everywhere a big disgrace,
Recycle, recycle, recycling bins.

Cans, paper, plastic bags,
Recycle, recycle, recycle everything.

Grace Forster (11)
The Avenue Primary School, Nunthorpe

War

Destruction of cities,
Bombing all around,
Bombing all around,
Bombing all around!
Sending precious people to war
And a hole in the ground
And a hole in the ground
And a hole in the ground.
Is it worth it at *all*?

Ground battles,
Air battles,
Sea battles,
Why choose war to settle your problems?

Would you go to war?

Matthew Wood (11)
The Avenue Primary School, Nunthorpe

Help!

One piece of litter can destroy our world,
So why don't you . . .
Pick it up!
Bin it!
Recycle it!
And show how much you care about our world.
One can could get caught in a boat's propeller
And break it so think before you throw it in the sea.
Think what you are doing to our world!
So save our world.

William Freeman (11)
The Avenue Primary School, Nunthorpe

Recycling!

Plastic bags dropped,
Cans crushed,
Bottles smashed,
Hurting all the animals,
Hurting all the world.

Plastic for our playground,
Cans for cars,
Bottles for milk,
Helping all the animals,
Helping all the world.

Recycling, recycling, recycling bins,
Recycle your cans,
Recycling, recycling, recycling bins,
Recycle your plastic bags,
Recycling, recycling, recycling bins,
Recycle your bottles.

Recycling!

Laura Simpson (11)
The Avenue Primary School, Nunthorpe

Litter

Dropping plastic bags, dropping plastic bags,
Strangles little animals,
Messes up the place,
We don't like it,
When dropping plastic bags, when dropping plastic bags!

Dropping leftover food, dropping leftover food
Makes the place unhygienic,
Sticks to the floor,
Sticks to your shoes,
When dropping leftover food, when dropping leftover food!

Dropping metal cans, dropping metal cans
Can hurt animals,
So please recycle,
Make the world a safer place for animals!

Jacob Segrave (11)
The Avenue Primary School, Nunthorpe

Make Our World A Better Place!

Smelly car fumes polluting the air,
Make our world less fair!

Graffiti spreading in places,
Please keep it away from little faces.

Destroying nature here and there, stop it!
Show that you really do care!

Thick, bright flames of fire,
Animals dying from barbed wire.

Cutting down trees, how sad -
You must be absolutely mad!

You really need to help
Save our world!

Rebecca Palmer (10)
The Avenue Primary School, Nunthorpe

How To Stop War!

We could make peace,
We could make peace,
By destroying guns and swords,
By destroying guns and swords,
And destroying war now,
And destroying war now.
Lives are lost,
Families are destroyed,
Stop war now!

If we make peace,
If we make peace,
And destroy guns and swords,
And destroy guns and swords,
Stopping war now,
Will make peace,
Will make peace.
No more lost lives,
No split-up families,
That's what will happen if we *stop war now!*
That's what will happen if we *stop war now!*

Alex Luke Morrell (10)
The Avenue Primary School, Nunthorpe

Thick Toxic Smoke

Thick toxic smoke
From chimneys tall,
Chavs that graffiti
On any alley wall.
It makes grannies batty,
It also looks tatty.
Cutting down a tree
Could kill a bee.
Do something,
Stop this from happening.

Joe Cairns (9)
The Avenue Primary School, Nunthorpe

Litter

Dropping plastic bags, dropping plastic bags
makes the place unhygienic
chokes and strangles animals
trust me, I have seen it

Dropping plastic bags, dropping plastic bags
there is one less bird
because of that bottle
oh please stop dropping plastic bags

Dropping plastic bags, dropping plastic bags
I'll clean it up
I'll clear the rats
I'll also save a lot of cats

No more plastic bags, no more plastic bags
You cleared it up
you put it away
so now the birds can fly away!

Matthew Bennison (11)
The Avenue Primary School, Nunthorpe

Help Our World

One shed kills a rainforest or maybe more,
Come on, help.
One piece of litter can affect our world,
Come on, help.
Chemical waste from factories is destroying the ozone layer,
Come on, help.
Car fumes polluting the air,
Come on, help.
Loads of rainforests are gone,
Change the world,
Come on, help!

Liam Reveley-Collins (9)
The Avenue Primary School, Nunthorpe

War

War is bad
war is bad
bloody murders in the land
bravery for the fans,
bravery for the fans,
bravery for the fans of war!

Evacuating people throughout the land
out the land
out the land without making a stand

People should rest in peace
rest in peace, rest in peace
but now they're dead in a trench

Down in the alley now I've shot
1 shot
2 shot
in the head
down he goes to the ground
bing bong bang now he's dead!

Ethan Walker (11)
The Avenue Primary School, Nunthorpe

Keep The World Alive

Forest fires destroy habitats killing trees,
It's a crime, they give out oxygen,
Without them we will die!

So recycle, if you don't recycle,
You will put the world at risk.

Graffiti destroys beautiful areas
Chemicals in the lakes kills animals
Gases from machines harm the world.

So recycle, if you don't recycle
You will put the world at risk.

Labib Uddin (11)
The Avenue Primary School, Nunthorpe

The Eco War

Let's all work together,
Make the future bright,
If we do it well,
We'll set it right.

Stripy skin on a model down the catwalk,
Stripy skin on a tiger down the stream.
Spotted feet on a woman down the high street,
Spotted feet on a leopard down the bay.

Let's all work together,
Make the future bright,
If we do it well,
We'll set it right.

Trees disappearing,
Homes disappearing,
Animals disappearing,
Is it worth it at all?

Let's all work together,
Make the future bright,
If we do it well,
We'll set it right.

Poachers are winning,
How can we stop them?
Let's try really hard
And see if we can drop them.

Let's all work together,
Make the future bright,
If we do it well,
We'll set it right.

Rebecca Jackson (11)
The Avenue Primary School, Nunthorpe

The Power Of Rainforests

Endangered creatures live there,
Being cut down quick,
Knowing all this really
Makes me sick.

Rainforests are great,
Don't deforestate.
Rainforests are great,
Don't deforestate.

More animals live
There than anywhere,
Yet lumberjacks
Keep going there.

Rainforests are great,
Don't deforestate,
Rainforests are great,
Don't deforestate.

Making paper and fire
By cutting down trees,
If we all try,
We can stop it at ease.

Rainforests are great,
Don't deforestate,
Rainforests are great,
Don't deforestate.

Matthew James Bradley (10)
The Avenue Primary School, Nunthorpe

Not Recycling?

Not recycling? Start recycling!
Come on . . . show you care!
Destruction of animals' habitats,
Destruction of forest homes,
One shed could kill a forest,
So leave them all alone.
Not recycling? Start recycling!
Come on . . . show you care.
You can make our world a better place
And not destroy the human race,
So . . .
Not recycling? Start recycling!
Come on and show you care.

Lucy Chambers (10)
The Avenue Primary School, Nunthorpe

Racism!

If you taunt,
It will haunt.

>   Racism!

Don't tease,
You aim not to please.

>   Racism!

It's definitely not charming,
It might even lead to self-harming.

>   Racism!

If you're not nice,
You will pay the price.

Racism! What can you do to stop it?

Katie Iley (11)
The Avenue Primary School, Nunthorpe

Why Not Help?

Just one piece of litter
Can affect several animals, so . . .
Why not help the planet?
And pick up litter -
Don't you know how long it takes
For plastic to rot away?
Thousands of years . . .
So . . .
Why not help the planet?
Pick up the plastic.
Just one shed can kill a forest, so . . .
Why not help the planet?
Use a plastic shed!

Joe Morley (11)
The Avenue Primary School, Nunthorpe

Do Your Part

Yobs destroy the trees
And it kills the bees so
Prevent destruction!
Do your part!
Spread the message!

If you don't recycle
You put the world in danger so
Prevent destruction!
Do your part!
Spread the message!

We use wood for boats,
Sheds and garages so
Prevent destruction!
Do your part!
Spread the message!

Recycle!

Luke Goddard (10)
The Avenue Primary School, Nunthorpe

Show You Care

Don't graffiti it affects your street
I'm sure a policeman you wouldn't wanna meet
So don't do it!
Never do it!
Show you care!

Don't use a big engined boat as it pollutes our seas!
If you do then you've gotta deal with me
So don't do it!
Never do it!
Show you care!

Pick up dog waste it can kill your kid!
If you don't then you'll have to pay a fine to sid!
So don't do it!
Never do it!
Show you care!

Don't graffiti!
Don't pollute!
Clean up!
You've gotta care!

Philippa Elizabeth Stone (10)
The Avenue Primary School, Nunthorpe

Show That You Care!

Cutting down trees,
Swaying in the breeze -
Recycle paper,
Make more paper.
Destroying habitats,
Please don't do that.
Recycle paper,
Don't cut down the trees.

One piece of litter,
Affects our world,
Pick it up,
To help our world.
Leaving pet waste,
Is a horrible way,
To not care -
Pick it up,
Help our world.
Don't pollute the air,
Show that you care,
Please, show that you care.

Molly Ryan (9)
The Avenue Primary School, Nunthorpe

Don't Litter

If you don't recycle you could change the world - so,
Put it away! Don't toss it away! Recycle it!
Animals die because we litter - so,
Put it away! Don't toss it away! Collect it up!

Don't drop litter around the place!
It is such a disgrace,
It takes ages to rot away!

Don't just throw it into seas,
It will kill fish species!
All you gotta do is put it away, don't toss it away, put it in a bin!
Animals get trapped in cans so,
Put it away! Don't toss it away! Put it in a recycle bin!

It will take centuries to rot!
All we gotta do is pick it up!
Then we can save our world.

Emily Heslington (10)
The Avenue Primary School, Nunthorpe

Recycle, Recycle, Recycle

First you write on a piece of paper,
Fill one side, use the other,
Now you can't use it as scrap, so . . .

Recycle, recycle, recycle,
Recycling's all it takes!
Just recycle, recycle, recycle,
You and me can save the world!
None of us want to waste trees,
Because we need a lot of oxygen in the air,
Do all you can, just . . .

Recycle, recycle, recycle,
Recycling's all it takes!
Just recycle, recycle, recycle,
You and me can save the world!

Rebecca Anne Moy (10)
The Avenue Primary School, Nunthorpe

Litter

One piece of litter can affect our world,
So pick it up, don't just throw it away.
Animals are dying from suffocation by litter,
So pick it up, don't just throw it away.
Some things take centuries to rot,
So pick them up, don't just throw them away.
Animals' habitats are at risk,
So pick it up, don't just throw it away.
Recycle, don't litter. Can you see the causes?
Recycle, don't litter. Can you see the causes?
Recycle, don't litter. Can you see the causes?
So pick it up, don't just throw it away.

Alexa Jayne Singleton (9)
The Avenue Primary School, Nunthorpe

Help The World!

People leave taps on - and that wastes water,
How can we help?
Turn taps off when you don't use them,
That will help!
Car fumes pollute the air,
How can we help?
Walk if you can and don't drive,
That will help!
Only one piece of litter affects our world,
How can we help?
Put all your litter in a bin,
That will help!
But don't put things which can be recycled in a normal bin,
Recycle everything you can!
That will help!

Abbie May Rodgers (10)
The Avenue Primary School, Nunthorpe

Save Our Planet

Animals suffer because of litter
Pollution causing animals to leave their habitats
Fires starting to grow because of factories
Pick up
Recycle
Save our planet

Graffiti destroys our local area
Stop, think about what you're doing
Don't throw litter into the sea
Cutting down trees is a bad idea
Pick up
Recycle
Save our planet

Seeing our bushes full of rubbish
I want to do something
If you throw anything away pick it up again!
Do something about it!

Rachel Harrison (10)
The Avenue Primary School, Nunthorpe

Destroying The World

A car?
All it does is poison the Earth -
It causes global warming -
Now . . .
Do you want this to happen?
No?
Then - take a walk,
Ride your bike
Or even recycle your car!
Chewing gum?
All it does is rot your teeth
And damage the look of the place -
So . . .
Please, put it in the bin
Or in the compost bin.
Will you do this now?
You know -
Pick up your rubbish
And change the world.

Ryan Derek Emmerson Iley (11)
The Avenue Primary School, Nunthorpe

The World Will Soon Vanish

War is bad,
War is bad,
Bloody murder in the land.

Bravery for fans,
Bravery for fans,
Bravery for fans of war.

War is bad,
War is bad,
Bloody murder in the land.

Evacuation for land,
Evacuation for land,
Killing like squashing a can.

War is bad,
War is bad,
Bloody murder in the land.

Sending tremendous people to land,
Sending tremendous people to land,
But no sight being seen.

War is bad,
War is bad,
Bloody murder in the land.

Would you fight in sad war?

Shafik Rehman (11)
The Avenue Primary School, Nunthorpe

Falling Trees

Trees are falling,
It's appalling.
Animals dying,
The birds will stop flying.

Model on the catwalk,
Leopard on the prey stalk,
Both wearing the same,
One life lost, one coat gained.

Trees are falling,
It's appalling.
Animals dying,
The birds will stop flying.

Fishermen going out,
Hoping to catch some trout.
Turtle gets caught,
By the hook with a fork.

Trees are falling,
It's appalling.
Animals dying,
The birds will stop flying.

Bethany Taylor (11)
The Avenue Primary School, Nunthorpe

Go Green!

There must be a simple solution,
For all the mass of pollution,
I urge your resistance
And don't take your car if your journey is short distance.
What is it with this war?
It should be against the law.
All this pain and all this death,
Every time you draw a breath.

All around there is litter,
It makes people bitter.
Do the world a favour, put stuff in the bin,
If you don't you'll be committing a sin.
All the rainforests are being cut down,
This is making people frown.
So recycle your paper for the best,
Because it's this abuse we detest!

Think of the people sleeping rough,
For them life is tough.
All of these people don't have a home
And forever these streets they will roam.
All the oil going into the sea,
Sounds pretty bad to me,
So just sit down and have a think
Because our world is on the brink!

Kaitlin Behan (10)
Trimdon Junior School, Trimdon Village

Recycle It

R ecycle things that you can
E verything you can recycle please do
C arry things out and put them in the recycling bin!
Y es recycle it
C ome on recycle
L augh while you recycle
E njoy recycling.

Laura Robson-Cross (8)
Trimdon Junior School, Trimdon Village

Litter, Litter

Litter, litter everywhere,
I look around it's always there.
Litter, litter everywhere,
People really just don't care!

Crisp packets,
Bubblegum,
Cola cans,
It's really scum.

Litter, litter everywhere,
I look around it's always there.
Litter, litter everywhere,
People really just don't care!

Plastic bags,
Magazines,
Finished fags,
Spoil the scenes.

It isn't hard,
To make places cleaner,
Pick up your rubbish,
Make this world greener.

Beth Donaldson & Ellie-Mae Flint (11)
Trimdon Junior School, Trimdon Village

Environmentally Friendly

Help us keep the streets clean,
By picking up your litter,
Then everyone will be pleased,
Instead of feeling bitter.

Help us to recycle things,
For a better place,
For the wildlife and the birds,
To be very, very safe.

Sophie Storey (8)
Trimdon Junior School, Trimdon Village

Will It Ever Stop?

Racism, is it fair?
Racism, do you care?
It doesn't matter whether you're black or white!
We still all have the same rights.

Recycling, do you do it?
Recycling, can you prove it?
Will you do it to help this world?
Together we can do it!

When will war ever stop?
Do you worry night and day?
Do you fear of getting shot?
Let's all turn another way!

If we all work together,
This world will be at peace!

Laura-Beth Mitchell (10)
Trimdon Junior School, Trimdon Village

Pollution Song

Dark chimneys pumping smoke
Making all the children choke
Toxic waste under the trees
Killing all the birds and bees.

Rivers full of deadly oil
Destroying fish with scales like foil
Cars and buses wasting fuel
Sometimes we can all be cruel.

For the future we must try
To reduce the planes that fly
Look after the Earth and all that's in it
Recycle rubbish, don't just bin it!

Lucy Atkinson (10)
Trimdon Junior School, Trimdon Village

Things Happening In The World

The oil has polluted the river by
transforming it to black,
like the midnight sky.

The wind roams through the land,
whoosh at unpredictable speeds,
blowing flowers and dispersing seeds.

They are as big as an aeroplane
and as loud as a cry.
They have a heart of gold
and they wouldn't hurt a fly.

Ben Pearson (10)
Whinstone Primary School, Ingleby Barwick

What We Don't See

They are as fast as a cheetah,
They still cannot outrun a gun,
Run, run, run;
Bang! goes the gun, one more drops dead,
All this is because we want to be fed.
We kill families without knowing,
Out hunting people are going,
We fill in a hole, little do we know it is a burrow,
Think of the family in sorrow,
Animals are teardrops,
As long as we are here they will sop.
This is what we don't see.

Jamie Connor (11)
Whinstone Primary School, Ingleby Barwick

Global Warming's Taking Its Toll!

People dying all around us,
Diseases spreading across the world,
Floods and cyclones destroy the globe,
People living in poverty,
Dying every second,
Global warming's taking its toll!

Deforestation, killing animals,
Industries creating CO_2,
Water levels are rising,
People are dying,
Global warming's taking its toll!

Two football pitches of trees,
Knocked down every 2 seconds,
World starvation spreading,
The planet is ending,
The atmosphere's filling up,
Global warming's taking its toll!

To save the world,
We must cut down on wood, electricity and CO_2,
We must do this immediately,
Before it's too late,
Let's stop global warming taking its toll!

Brett Hessing (11)
Whinstone Primary School, Ingleby Barwick

Save The World

A can could be a car,
A can could be a plane,
A can could be another can,
So save the world again!

Callum Frost & Joe Caygill (11)
Whinstone Primary School, Ingleby Barwick

Green Day Poem

G lobal warming is bad for the Earth
L ook and you will see
O r you can stop driving cars
B us is the way to get around
A nd stop lake pollution
L isten and you can do something

W arn everybody
A nd nobody will listen
R oaming across the dirty water
M issing lots of people
I n every different way
N ever do something wrong
G o and do the right thing to stop pollution.

Charlie Scales (11)
Whinstone Primary School, Ingleby Barwick

Global Warming

The oceans are rising,
So learn to swim,
Tsunamis are coming,
Things will get grim.

If we stop now,
We might survive,
1,000 years to come,
The Earth will go *kaboom!*

The world will become hell,
If we do not help,
If you just cycle,
It would be a great help.

Jack Bankhurst (10)
Whinstone Primary School, Ingleby Barwick

Pollution

P eople use too much electricity which will make the world die out.
O verflowing the sky with pollution we are still alive.
L ighting the sky with steam and dust.
L ighting the sky with rain and cloud.
U gly smog and smoke fill our sky,
T elling people to stop but they don't.
I wish I could do something to help the world.
O nly if we could help the world.
N ever will we stop trying to help.

Olivia Rich (11)
Whinstone Primary School, Ingleby Barwick

Flood

When it floods you're trapped inside
And lots of people might have died.
The rampaging water destroys the town,
People bobbing up and down,
Trying to hide from the dreadful flood,
Crashing hard as a rhino charging,
The crashing water looks like blood.

James Raymond Knott (11)
Whinstone Primary School, Ingleby Barwick

Animals

Every day animals die away,
All we do is sit and play.
As we sit and scoff our faces,
Some animals try to find comfy places.
We always go on holiday,
But animals can't find a place to stay.
I'm begging you please, stop chopping down trees.

Joseph Tomlin (11)
Whinstone Primary School, Ingleby Barwick

The Whale

W hales are in danger. Blue, humpback and northern.
H ere comes the oil! *Splodge! Splat! Gurgle!*
A s nasty chemicals pollute my home.
L eaving behind a stench that smells like dead bodies.
E els, penguins, gulls and dolphins too.
   Run for cover, away from the black blanket of doom!

Jack Horrocks (11)
Whinstone Primary School, Ingleby Barwick

Save The World

Everywhere, every day
People stop to think in their own way
Many children want to play
So let's shout out and play, say . . .
Stop cutting trees please, please
Please, help our world and save the day
So we can live happy in the summer, May
Let's stop it now but how?
Recycle cans, bottles, paper, plastic
That will be fantastic!

Abbie Manning (11)
Whinstone Primary School, Ingleby Barwick

Litter

L eft around the streets every day,
I n the sewers, blocking the drains,
T here in the dumping ground, wasting our land,
T he litter destroying our ozone layer,
E mpty ground, waiting to be filled,
R eady to be filled, to be destroyed.

Jack Christopher Thrower (11)
Whinstone Primary School, Ingleby Barwick

Whales!

All the whales are swimming in the sea
Swimming around just like me
They calm us down with their peaceful song
So why do they hunt them down in Hong Kong?

Some of the whales are swimming in the sea
They know it's not a safe place to be
But they can't run and they can't hide
So they have to stay as the hunters come to play

No whales are left in the sea swimming
So the hunters feel like they are winning
But the people of the world won't give up yet
Because some of them are being kept as a pet.

Georgia Helliwell (10)
Whinstone Primary School, Ingleby Barwick

The Black Death

Bang! Crash! Creak!
Trees go,
As humans destroy the forest,
Quicker than the black death,
Car exhaust fumes cough out poisonous gases like cyanide,
Killing animals,
Animals' homes destroyed,
For more human homes when they need no more,
We don't have homes only some,
Which are ready to be destroyed,
We can't stop the black death
Choking us,
Killing trees,
We have no homes now,
Please stop!

Zack Thomas (11)
Whinstone Primary School, Ingleby Barwick

Really Recycling

If you think you can get cash from old trash,
Instead of it being turned into ash,
You can get money from plastic,
That's why it's fantastic.
Why do people think recycling is junk?
Those people just act like punks!
Crash, bang, splat - they crush cans just like that,
Then we see the big crop of cans rotting in the ground
Like very old mud in a big pile of fat.
Our beautiful world ruined by people who throw cans into bins,
Faster than a basketball player!
People drop cans on the floor then say,
'Don't be troubled, someone will pick it up later . . .'

Jordan Martin (11)
Whinstone Primary School, Ingleby Barwick

Car Pollution

Car pollution is making our planet die,
before we know it we will be as black as the midnight sky.
Car pollution is making me sad,
before we know it the planet will go mad.
Car pollution is rotting the trees,
before they die they will take me.
Traffic, traffic everywhere,
but the silly old drivers they don't care.
Please, please let me talk,
please, please, please walk.
Come on, come on, clean our field,
don't let me get out my dusty old battle shield.

Evie Hollis (11)
Whinstone Primary School, Ingleby Barwick

Consequences!

Polluting our world, are vehicles and cars,
Wanting to go close places and far,
Housing estates are being built,
Flattening hills that were on a tilt.

Global warming is in the air,
All the sad news we have to share.
In the world is lots of smog,
Carbon dioxide but mainly fog.

The consequences for dropping litter,
Makes the world become unfitter.
Save electricity, pull the plug,
Do all this, the world is happy,
Give everyone a hug!

Sophie Patterson (11)
Whinstone Primary School, Ingleby Barwick

Global Warming

The animals flee,
As we cut down trees.
Their habitats disappear,
Under our big bulldozers,
We knock their forests over,
It isn't fair
And we should take more care,
Before animals and forests disappear!

Sarah McCarthy (11)
Whinstone Primary School, Ingleby Barwick

Save The World!

S mog is a combination of carbon and fog
A nimals and humans may never live again
V ery good the world is now
E verything will get better soon.

T he world can be saved right now
H ear the sound of extinction coming near
E verybody's quivering with fear.

W atch global warming coming close
O r do something right now
R ule our world we are all in charge
L ove our universe do something today
D on't stand back do something *now!*

Amber Khan (11)
Whinstone Primary School, Ingleby Barwick

Pollution

All the gas from the cars killing life,
Harming living animals and humans.
The smoking affecting people causing death,
The oil as black as ebony spilling into the sea.
Gulp, gulp, gulp, it spreads like a blanket,
The fishes are floating and the whales are sinking.
The gases from the boats need to stop,
They are causing pollution to places nearby.

Abdul Hamid Rauf (10)
Whinstone Primary School, Ingleby Barwick

Save The World

Cars are driving past my bed,
The fumes are getting in my head.
The light bulb flickers light and dim,
Trying to keep the dying light in.

In fifty years' time, my gran says there'll be
No Scarborough, no Devon and no Whitby.
But if this will happen,
I guess we'll just see.

The penguins are yearning for sea and for ice,
If they all die out, it won't be nice.
The polar bears are hungry, starving to be precise,
They eat fish, not grains of rice.

The animals are crying for their home they once had,
The modern culture is making rainforests bad.
The trees are chopped down, it's driving them mad,
The animals and plants are mourning, they're sad.

The world is slowly dying,
Save the world before it's too late . . .

Sonia Mansouri (11)
Whinstone Primary School, Ingleby Barwick

The Whales' Poem

Don't hurt the whales, they haven't hurt you,
Would you like it if the whales killed you?
You can kill a fish,
Then cook it and place it on a dish.
Just because whales are sea creatures,
Doesn't mean you can kill the poor creatures.
So don't hurt the whales,
You can kill something that has scales!

Corinne Kerr (10)
Whinstone Primary School, Ingleby Barwick

Extinction

Some animals become extinct
Animals will be gone by the time I blink
Fish going down the kitchen sink
The shiny blue whale covered in ink
It looks like a layer of treacle
What are you doing about this problem?

Elephants threatened and endangered
The dodo bird is gone
All that is left is the memories, bone and skin
Animals extinct: oh a human sin
What are you doing about this problem?

Lots of animals becoming extinct
Animals will be gone by the time I blink
My fish went down the kitchen sink
The shiny blue whale was covered in ink
It was as graceful as a swan
What shall we do about this problem?

Daisy Hearfield (11)
Whinstone Primary School, Ingleby Barwick

Floods

F resh water being wasted because of us
L ives are lost for the cost
O r people are becoming injured
O verflowing water in the city centre
D eep as the ocean-blue sea
S ome people are destroying the world.

Mathew Clasper (10)
Whinstone Primary School, Ingleby Barwick

Elephant Life!

As the sun comes up to shine
The elephants know it's time
To stomp around and play
And eat and drink all day

But as the sun goes down
The elephants look around
As they cuddle up tight
And sleep all through the night

The sun has gone
But there is footprints of someone
They are here
The elephants fear
They shouldn't have to.

Rachel Stabler (11)
Whinstone Primary School, Ingleby Barwick

Eco - Haikus

Animals

Animal skin worn,
Animals should not be killed,
They are innocent!

Electricity

Turn the lights off now,
Global warming, such a threat,
Earth is forever!

Wars

Guns sound, people scream,
Needless fighting on our Earth,
End the fighting now!

Ben Doherty (11)
Whinstone Primary School, Ingleby Barwick

The World's Terror

Crack! Crunch!
It crumbles down
It falls down on a humble town
Terror and destruction all around
With vicious cracks in the ground
Houses crack, break in two
Who will help them? Who, who?
Earthquakes rattle, shake and break
Children lying down with an ache
We can help if we just try
Otherwise people will die!

Luke Parkin (11)
Whinstone Primary School, Ingleby Barwick

Save The Planet

Save the planet by . . .

   S ave electricity,
   A nimal breeding programs,
   V alue of plastic bags,
   E nvironmentally friendly.

   T rees being left alone,
   H elp plants grow,
   E ducation is the key.

   W alk to school,
   O ff goes your computer,
   R ecycle,
   L ights turned off,
   D on't travel in a car as much.

Bethany Clay (11)
Whinstone Primary School, Ingleby Barwick

Save Our World

S witch off lights in empty rooms
A TV on standby? Switch it off!
V alue our energy - it's costing the Earth
E nergy wasted in lots of homes

T ry to pick up litter
H orrid sights of litter on the ground
E veryone pick up litter and you'll be fitter!

P eople all around making an effort
L iving the life of recycling
A ll things that are recycled are made into something new
N early everyone trying
E very day people are recycling
T o try and save the planet.

Fenella Pinkney (11)
Whinstone Primary School, Ingleby Barwick

Save Our Earth

Do you want the Earth to die?

Chopping down the rainforests,
Causes animals to die,
Chopping down the rainforests,
Means there's less oxygen to survive.

Environmental pollution,
We have to help stop,
Environmental pollution,
Destroys our world.

Do you want the Earth to die?

Mariko Yanagisawa (11)
Whinstone Primary School, Ingleby Barwick

The Terror Of The Earth

Terror swirls in the air
The vicious cyclone brings a scare
Other countries just don't care
They're all happy it's not fair.

They're left with nothing, nothing at all
Vicious cracks in the walls
Houses crack into two
Who will save them, what can we do?

People cry in pain
They haven't got skilled doctors, what a shame
These Earth hazards are terribly unfair.

Daniel Gavaghan (11)
Whinstone Primary School, Ingleby Barwick

Fire!

Save the world?
Walking past the dirty street,
In England global warming has made heat.
Ice caps burnt by the sun,
Now the polar bears can't have fun.

Light is everywhere in town,
No dark today, lots of people frown.
Electricity is powerful, electricity is huge,
World is shrinking, electricity is growing . . .
Save the world!

Grace Autumn Patricia Riley (11)
Whinstone Primary School, Ingleby Barwick

Earth's Energy

Earth's energy gone,
Everybody's panicking,
Everything is gone,
TVs are left on all day,
Power is used fast!

The future is a mystery,
The world is on edge,
Everything left is bound to die,
Save the world,
Turn off!

Jay Collier (10)
Whinstone Primary School, Ingleby Barwick

Lungs Of The Earth

The lungs of the Earth
The rainforests are being chopped down
Their future looks bleak
A tree for a seed
Stop the deforestation
Let the Earth's lungs breathe.

Christopher Dodds (11)
Whinstone Primary School, Ingleby Barwick

Save The Earth

Save our planet
It is soon to be destroyed,
War rules it,
The homeless are begging,
Global warming will destroy the ice caps,
Rainforests are being cut down,
You can help.
Help the Earth today!

Logan Brennan (10)
Whinstone Primary School, Ingleby Barwick

Save Our World Today

Do you want to save the world?

Environmental pollution
Causes the Earth's temperature to rise.
Environmental pollution,
Gives no prize.

Destroying the rainforest
Means less chance to survive.
Destroying the rainforest
Means there's no home for animals.

Do you want to save the world?

Sonia Hussein (11)
Whinstone Primary School, Ingleby Barwick

Global Warming Scares

Smog surrounding town,
People wearing frowns,
Citizens always sad,
Pollution's really bad.

World is getting hot,
Scientists in a knot,
Save electricity now,
Everyone . . . act now!

Polar caps are going,
Eskimos must start rowing.
The penguins are all dying,
Mothers and children crying!

Stop global warming now!

Danny Barry (11)
Whinstone Primary School, Ingleby Barwick

Young Writers Information

We hope you have enjoyed reading this book - and that you will continue to enjoy it in the coming years.

If you like reading and writing poetry drop us a line, or give us a call, and we'll send you a free information pack.

Alternatively if you would like to order further copies of this book or any of our other titles, then please give us a call or log onto our website at
www.youngwriters.co.uk

Young Writers Information
Remus House
Coltsfoot Drive
Peterborough
PE2 9JX

(01733) 890066